D1503834

*The*

PLEASURE OF GARDENING

VEGETABLES,
HERBS & FRUIT

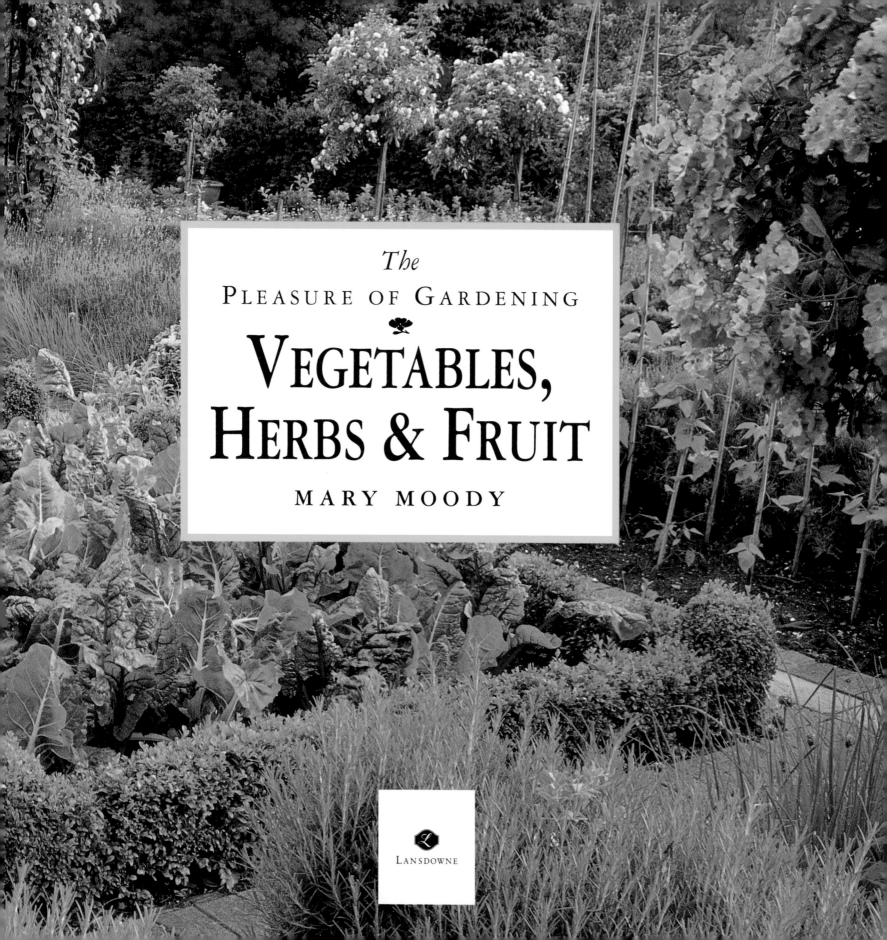

*The*
PLEASURE OF GARDENING

VEGETABLES,
HERBS & FRUIT

MARY MOODY

LANSDOWNE

# CONTENTS

# The
# KITCHEN
# GARDEN

*ABOVE: A well organised and orderly vegetable garden is a visual treat, with neat rows of healthy crops in various stages of maturity, from seedlings to those awaiting harvest.*

*PREVIOUS PAGE: The herb parsley (*Petroselinum crispum*) is good value for space, needing very little room to grow, yet producing foliage that is extremely high in vitamins and minerals.*

# A Brief History

The first gardeners were thought to have started scratching at the earth's surface ten thousand years ago, laying the foundations of agriculture and horticulture that gradually spread throughout the world. Those early exponents were centred in the Middle East, South-East Asia and Central America; however over a period of several thousand years their skills crept westward through the Mediterranean, north into Europe and eventually to Britain. As early as 2400 BC settlers in Britain imported domesticated animals and seeds, although their skills were less sophisticated than those practised around the Mediterranean.

In Roman times many 'fruits of the field' that we enjoy today were being grown in abundance, including turnips, radishes, beans, basil, garlic, asparagus, cabbages, lettuce, endive, chicory, melons and gourds. Herbs were also widely grown for both medicinal and culinary purposes.

Historically the rise and fall of horticulture has depended on the prevailing social environment. During the Dark Ages, for example, knowledge and practice of epicurean gardening virtually died out in Britain.

In the New World there is evidence that quite advanced gardening techniques were being used in Central America as far back as seven thousand years. Plants such as potatoes, maize, sweet peppers, kidney beans, Jerusalem

*The garden as an artform, with carefully grouped rows of leafy herbs arranged in formal patterns. A garden of this scope is obviously very time consuming and labour-intensive.*

artichokes and tomatoes travelled to Europe from this part of the world.

Today there is a constant flow of seed material across cultural boundaries, with exotic and unusual varieties from South-East Asia being grown side by side with traditional European staples. Many seed producers are going back to old-fashioned, non-hybridised varieties, as gardeners seek the nostalgia of the traditional cottage 'kitchen garden'. While mass production of food over the past six decades has reduced the individual vegetable plot, there is still a trend in some western countries for people to grow at

least some of their produce in their own backyard gardens.

Travelling across Europe by train provides evidence of enthusiastic gardeners growing a wide range of produce in small holdings along the railway verges. In Britain the system of garden 'allotments' still occurs, and enthusiasts travel to their plot of land to reap the benefits of their labours.

In countries with a greater land mass, such as America and Australia, most home-owners have a sizeable plot of land surrounding the family home, and this gives scope for the growing of many productive crops.

There are various reasons why we choose to incorporate a vegetable, herb or fruit garden into our landscape. The increasing cost of living prompts some to start a kitchen garden, while others are disenchanted with the widespread use of pesticides and herbicides and the lack of flavour and texture in food that has been mass produced and kept for long periods in cold storage while being transported.

Times of economic hardship bring a rapid increase in this style of home self-sufficiency. During the Great Depression of the early 1930s many families survived out of their gardens, with the addition of a few chickens to provide meat, eggs and necessary manure.

*Vegetables, Herbs and Fruit* explores all the possibilities for creating a flourishing and productive kitchen garden.

# Garden Location

To be productive, a vegetable plot must be located in the sunniest part of the garden. While vegetables appreciate some protection from prevailing winds, they should not be located too close to large established trees, which will compete for nutrients and cast shadows that block precious sunlight.

The most common position for a home vegetable garden is in the centre of the main back garden, behind the house. The term 'kitchen garden' implies that the garden is within easy access of the kitchen door, where in the late afternoon 'the cook' can quickly dash out and gather fresh greens and herbs for the evening meal. It is for this reason that many modern gardeners have abandoned the vegetable plot; it became too visually prominent, and at various times too labour intensive to maintain neatly. It was often replaced with an outdoor entertaining area and barbeque!

When deciding on a suitable location, take into consideration soil drainage as well as aspect and wind protection. Planting a low to medium-size hedge around the vegetable garden—black and red currant bushes are excellent—will certainly provide an effective windbreak at ground level, while not blocking the sunlight.

A garden that is located beside a wall or fence can be very productive, providing the wall is on the northside (northern hemisphere gardens) or the southside (southern hemisphere gardens). The wall not only provides a backdrop for the growing of climbing vegetables such as runner (pole) beans or cucumbers, but if made of stone or brick it will absorb and intensify the warmth of the sun, creating a microclimate. In tropical areas the heat may become too intense, but certainly in cool or cold climates a garden bedded in front of a warm wall will produce better results!

## DRAINAGE

Poor drainage can be a problem, and it's one that should be addressed prior to planting out the garden. To test the ground for adequate drainage first dig a hole to a depth of 30 cm (1 ft) then fill it with water. The speed with which this water drains away will determine the drainage quality of the bed. If water is retained in the hole for more than 30 minutes some corrective steps must be taken.

RIGHT: *The ideal location for a vegetable plot is the sunniest place in the garden, with some protection against strong winds in the form of a wall, trellis or windbreak.*

*ABOVE: A neat edging of treated timber logs allows the soil to be built up above ground level with organic matter to correct inadequate drainage.*
*OPPOSITE: A terraced wall of stone creates a warm micro-climate for the growing of vegetables and herbs, acting both as a windbreak and a suntrap.*

The most inexpensive method of correcting poor drainage is to create raised beds i.e. beds above ground level. This can be done using timber or bricks as an edging material, then incorporating lots of organic matter (straw, manure, compost) to improve the texture and drainage qualities of the soil.

The alternative method is to lay some underground drainage pipes to take excess moisture away from the garden bed. This may need to be done with expert advice, although the advent of lightweight plastic underground drainage pipes has certainly made the task easier and less expensive.

# STYLE OPTIONS

# The Flower Garden

In many instances fruits, vegetables and herbs can be integrated into the general garden landscape instead of being grown in a specific location set aside for the purpose. This method is good for people who have little or no garden space, or for those whose gardens are very shady, and open sunny space is at a premium.

Providing the growing conditions are suitable, it is easy to create a successful mixed garden bed of annuals, perennials and shrubs together with vegetables and herbs. Indeed many vegetables and herbs are highly decorative, adding colour and texture to the garden as well as providing a valuable source of nutrients!

## REQUIREMENTS
Because plenty of sunshine is essential for the growing of most vegetables and herbs, a garden bed located in full sun

*OPPOSITE: Shrubs, herbs and perennials can be combined successfuly in a more formal landscape, with plants selected according to their foliage and flower colour and texture for a harmonious result.*

*PREVIOUS PAGE: The nodding mauve flowerheads of chives (Allium schoenoprasum) can look attractive when incorporated into a flower garden. Chives are also well suited to container cultivation.*

will be perfect for combining flowering and productive species. If the intention is to fill spaces between flowering plants with vegetables or herbs, then good soil conditions will also be needed to provide sufficient nutrients. Most vegetables are quite demanding and should be grown quickly and given plenty of space to avoid tough, inedible results. Therefore the soil will need to be enriched with plenty of well-rotted manure or compost prior to planting, and in many cases a liquid fertiliser or dried plant food (such as poultry manure pellets or dried cow manure) should be added as a side dressing.

Some plants will need the support of a garden stake or trellis, and this should be taken into account before planting. Ideally, taller species should be planted towards the back of the garden bed or border, with lower growing species positioned towards the front.

## FRUIT TREES
Many fruiting varieties of trees can be planted instead of ornamental trees. As a garden feature, use deciduous fruit trees such as apples, plums, peaches, apricots or nectarines, all of which are valued for their delightful spring blossoms as well as for their fruit. When using fruiting varieties, avoid pruning hard as would be done in the orchard, as this will detract

# The Flower Garden

*A*t first glance this appears to be a classical mixed perennial border, however a variety of vegetables and herbs have been integrated with the flowers for an eye-catching and appetising effect. Many herbs, in particular, have interesting and unusual foliage and the same growth habits and requirements as ornamental perennials. As with any border planting, taller species should be positioned at the back of the garden, with groundcovering varieties located at the front.

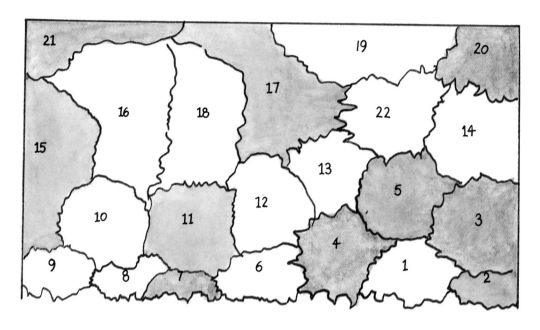

## Key to planting scheme

1. Mint (*Mentha*) a perennial herb with many varieties and foliage colours, growing to 60cm (2ft).

2. Alyssum (*Lobularia maritimum*) a low-growing, flowering annual to 20cm (8in) with white, pink or purple flowers.

3. Sorrell (*Rumex scutatus*) a leafy annual herb growing to 45cm (18in).

4. Spinach (*Spinacia oleracea*) a leafy vegetable growing to 45cm (18in).

5. Marigolds (*Tagetes*) a colourful annual growing to 50cm (1ft 8in) are also a good organic insect repellent.

6. Basil (*Ocimum basilicum*) a leafy annual herb growing to 75cm (2ft 6in).

7. Lobelia (*Lobelia erinus*) a low-growing annual to 15cm (6in) with bright blue/purple flowers.

8. Thyme (*Thymus vulgaris*) a low-growing perennial herb to 30cm (1ft) with fragrant grey-green foliage.

9. Sage (*Salvia officinalis*) a perennial herb growing to 90cm (3ft) with rough, grey-green foliage.

10. Camomile (*Matricaria chamomilla*) a pretty perennial herb growing to 60cm (2ft) with white daisy flowers.

11. Chives (*Allium schoenoprasum*) forms a clump to 30cm (1ft) of grass-like foliage topped with globular mauve flowerheads.

13. Carrots (*Daucus carota*) a root vegetable with feathery foliage growing to 30cm (1ft).

14. Dill (*Anethum graveolens*) a tall-growing annual herb, reaching 90cm (3ft) in height.

15. Lavender (*Lavandula spica*) an evergreen shrub to 50cm (1ft 8in) with grey-green foliage and fragrant lavender flowers.

16. Kniphofia (*Kniphofia uvaria*) a flowering perennial growing to 120cm (4ft) with slender stems topped by bright orange-red flowers.

17. Artichokes (*Cynara scolymus*) a leafy vegetable growing to 120cm (4ft).

18. Foxgloves (*Digitalis purpurea*) an old-fashioned perennial that can reach 1.5m (5ft) with pink-purple flowers.

20. Delphiniums (*Delphinium ajacus*) a flowering perennial growing to 90cm (3ft).

21. Climbing beans (*Phaseolus coccineus*) a climbing vegetable reaching 2m (6ft) and needing a trellis support.

22. Dutch Iris (*I. xiphium x I. tingitana*) flowering bulbs growing to 45cm (18 in) with colourful flowers borne on spikes.

from the natural line and shape of the tree. Instead prune lightly only in winter, removing dead wood and cutting back branches that would hang to the ground if laden with fruit.

Small fruiting bushes such as currants or blueberries are also of great ornamental value. Ideal for cold climates, they make an excellent small deciduous hedge, and as a bonus produce delicious, vitamin-rich berries in late spring. Every garden in frost-free areas should have a lemon tree, and this can be easily positioned at the back of a flower bed or in a large tub near a verandah or patio. Not only are the fruit a valuable source of vitamin C, but their glossy green foliage and fragrant blossoms make the tree itself a delight.

## HERBS

Herbs are probably the easiest plants to successfully integrate into the flower garden. Tall stalks of dill, fennel or garlic look dramatic at the back of a cottage garden border, while shrubby camomile and rosemary are valuable plants in their own right. Low-growing thyme is a perfect fragrant ground-cover, and the mints can be combined to provide a wonderful array of foliage colours and textures. Other herb basics such as parsley and chives are also attractive in a mixed garden or grown in a terracotta pot in a sunny, sheltered situation.

## VEGETABLES

There are many vegetables that will enhance the flower garden with beautiful foliage colours and textures. The full range of lettuce, including those with red or pale green leaves, look marvellous

planted between bulbs or annuals. Beetroot (beets), which have deep green tops veined with brilliant red, can be used in a clump as a feature plant. Cauliflowers and cabbages can also be grown between shrubs and perennials providing they are well fed and well watered, and climbing beans can be used as a feature when grown against a wall or fence at the back of the garden.

*ABOVE: Although in separate beds, the lettuces (*Lactuca sativa) *are not out of place in an area of the garden otherwise reserved for ornamentals.*

*RIGHT: Many herbs such as yarrow (*Achillea millefolium) *and rosemary (*Rosmarinus officinalis) *are shrubs or clump-forming, making them ideal for placement in a perennial border.*

# The Organic Garden

Those wishing to create an organic garden should first responsibly dispose of all cans or bottles of herbicides or pesticides. At times it is tempting to reach for the 'quick fix' of a chemical, but although this will solve problems in the short term, they will recur unless preventative steps are taken.

Planning an organic vegetable garden involves looking at the existing growing conditions and endeavouring to maximise the natural attributes of the location. Organic gardens should aim to create balance by allowing all the natural forces to co-exist harmoniously. Instead of eradicating pests with chemical sprays, predators such as birds should be encouraged into the garden, creating biological control. The successful organic garden will therefore eventually become a small, self-sustaining ecosystem.

In the long term an organic garden should be able to keep itself going with-

*LEFT: Gardeners who choose alternatives to chemical sprays and fertilisers do so for health and ecological reasons. The results are very rewarding.*

out imported materials although, initially, organic soil builders such as manures may be required to increase the soil fertility and improve its texture.

Composting is a very important aspect of organic gardening, and a well-planned garden will have provision for the recycling of all organic materials. It is a good idea to set aside one area within the garden for composting directly on the ground, and then to use this area for planting once the compost heap has broken down. This is not only labour—saving, but will also ensure that all parts of the garden benefit from the additional earthworm activity if the heap can be positioned in a different place every time.

Serious organic gardeners often invest in a 'shredding' machine which is used to finely chop organic materials such as leaves, bark, fine branches and spent plants. By reducing the size of the organic matter the composting process is greatly hastened. This shredded material also makes an excellent surface layer mulch and ensures that nothing useful is wasted.

## The Organic Garden

*T*he basic principles of companion planting are essential in the organic vegetable garden, where plants will rely strongly on the support and protection of other species. Plants must have the optimum growing conditions to withstand disease and pest infestation. The quality of the soil is of primary importance and time must be spent improving the texture and drainage, and ensuring that the essential nutrients are available.

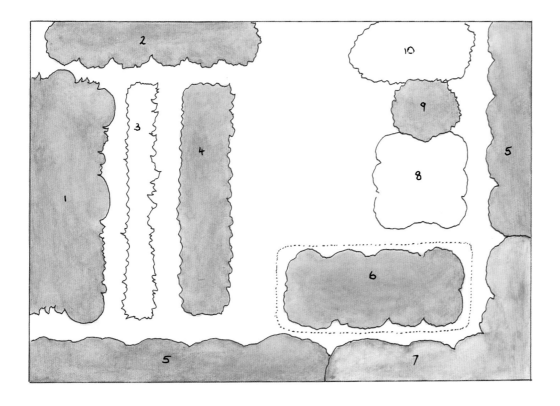

## Key to planting scheme

1. Sweet corn (*Zea mays*) is a tall plant and should be placed at the back of the garden. It shades the fruits of the pumpkin (*Curcubita*).

2. Pumpkin (*Cucurbita*) has broad leaves to shade the exposed roots of the corn (*Zea mays*).

3. Chives (*Allium schoenoprasum*) are strongly aromatic, exuding a scent that repels insects.

4. Carrot (*Daucus carota*) is a non-demanding root crop that should be followed by a leaf crop such as spinach (*Spinacia oleracea*).

5. Marigolds (*Tagetes*) not only help to discourage certain insects, but they also exude substances from their roots that destroy soil nematodes.

6. Lettuce (*Lactuca sativa*) seedlings can be surrounded by sawdust to protect them against snails and slugs.

7. Nasturtiums (*Tropaeolum* ) are useful for attracting aphids away from fruits and vegetables, and also discouraging white fly.

8. Cabbage (*Brassica oleracea* var. *capitata*) a demanding crop that must be well mulched with well rotted manure.

9. Rosemary (*Rosmarinus officinalis*) has fragrant foliage which can be harvested and made into an insect-repelling spray.

10. A compost heap, when built in the vegetable garden, is easily spread and planted over after decomposition.

11. Tomatoes (*Lycopersicon esculentum*) are good companion plants to grow beside basil (*Ocimum basilicum*).

12. Basil (*Ocimum basilicum*) needs full sun and well drained soil, and helps to keep tomatoes (*Lycopersicon esculentum*) healthy. Interestingly the two are also frequently combined in cooking!

The most important change to make when planning an organic vegetable garden is a change of attitude. Consumers have come to expect perfection in the food they eat—no blemishes, no unshapely bumps. In an organic garden there is room to accommodate the odd failure, the odd crop loss, the odd competition with insects.

Prevention is the key to success. A healthy crop, grown in healthy fertile soil will be resistant to attack by pests or diseases. Choose vegetables that are right for your climate, and plant them at the correct time of the year. Keep weeds down by regular mulching and feed plants to ensure steady growth. In these conditions plants will thrive, and problems be kept to a minimum.

Follow the principles of crop rotation and companion planting to keep the garden healthy and productive. This is important when establishing a garden layout. Position together plants that complement each other, and incorporate species that repel insects.

Simple tricks like sprinkling sawdust around lettuce will help to keep snails and slugs away. (They hate the texture of sawdust, and will not cross this barrier!)

Check the garden daily, as many problems can be averted if detected in the early stages. Look at the back of leaves for signs of infestation, and manually remove pests rather than spray.

*RIGHT: A dramatic formal organic vegetable and herb garden, where mulch is used to suppress weed growth and organic manures have been applied to keep plants growing at a steady pace.*

# The Permaculture Garden

This garden style is essentially organic, but it involves certain design aspects that make it unique. Permaculture is a system that evolved in Australia, and although it is best known in arid regions of the world where lush, productive gardens have been built on ground that was once barren, its basic precepts are still useful in more fertile regions.

The design features of the permaculture garden take into consideration climate and aspect of the garden, naturally requiring maximum sun and certain wind protection. Crops vary according to the climate, and planting also varies to cope with winters that suffer severe frosts, or tropical climates where summer crops can 'bolt to seed'.

In the garden overview a simple permaculture plan has been designed for the average, medium-to-large back garden. The garden includes the following features.

**1. At the kitchen step** Plant a lemon or lime tree here (only in frost-free areas, or plant in containers indoors to protect in winter) and the frequently picked herbs (parsley, oregano, mint) plus salad greens (lettuces, salad burnet).

**2. The herb garden** This is effective as a raised bed edged with bricks or timber, and designed as spiral incorporating rocks which provide good drainage for culinary herbs such as chives, basil, thyme, marjoram and rosemary.

**3. Clipping beds** For more frequently used herbs and salad greens that are grown in quantity, such as shallots, cress, dandelion and corn salad.

**4. Pathside plucking vegetables** Create easy access to long-bearing vegetables by planting them alongside paths. This gives easy access to useful vegetables such as silverbeet (Swiss chard), spinach, celery, fennel, cos (Romaine) lettuce and various herbs, that are continuously harvested by cutting or pulling off leaves or fruits.

**5. Keyhole beds** These are space saving when carefully designed, with larger plant varieties at the back providing suntraps and windbreaks for smaller and more sensitive vegetables and herbs. This is the ideal position for growing tomatoes.

**6. Narrow beds** These allow easy access for the harvesting of plants that require a long period of picking, for example beans, peas, tomatoes, eggplants, carrots, zucchini and companion herbs.

**7. Broader beds** These are suited to slower maturing, bulk harvested crops such as corn, pumpkins, melons, onions, potatoes, turnips, swedes, rutabagas and companion herbs. Grains and pulses can also be grown here if space permits.

**8. Vine and trellis crops** Trellises make space for growing climbing beans, peas, chokos, grapes and other climbing varieties. Support could also be provided by a pergola over a garden path or vine arbour.

**9. Garden pond** A pond can be simply formed by using an old truck or tractor tyre. Water chestnuts, water lilies with edible roots, and watercress can be grown in it with perhaps a few fish included.

**10. Fruit trees and poultry** Where space is limited, fruiting trees can be trained as espalier forms against walls. Poultry runs beneath fruiting trees are good because the birds keep insects under control.

Permaculture gardens are also characterised by the use of non-hybridised seeds for propagation. A percentage of each crop is allowed to 'go to seed' and the seeds are then allowed to scatter and emerge wherever they have fallen. This naturally self-sustaining method considerably reduces the planning and planting time.

*RIGHT: Against a woodland backdrop, a recently established permaculture garden is shown, with beds laid out according to the basic design principles, and taking into consideration companion planting and crop rotation.*

# The Permaculture Garden

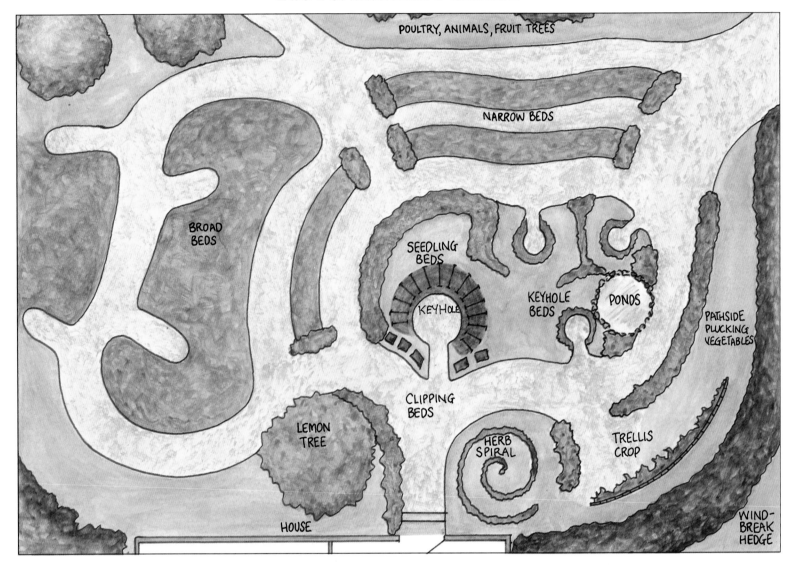

POULTRY, ANIMALS, FRUIT TREES

NARROW BEDS

BROAD BEDS

SEEDLING BEDS

KEYHOLE

KEYHOLE BEDS

PONDS

PATHSIDE PLUCKING VEGETABLES

CLIPPING BEDS

LEMON TREE

HERB SPIRAL

TRELLIS CROP

HOUSE

WIND-BREAK HEDGE

*P*ermaculture landscapes, (*above*) are based on specific design principles, to allow for low maintenance productive gardening. Fruits, vegetables and herbs are grown organically, taking advantage of every available resource. Part of the rationale is to make the garden easy to access, with frequently used herbs located near the kitchen door, and plants grouped together according to their harvesting periods. Certain plants are allowed to seed and self-sow for new crops the following season.

*I*n keyhole beds, (*right*) plants are grouped together to provide protection and support for each other.

## Key to planting scheme

1. Jerusalem artichokes (*Helianthus tuberosus*) are an easy-to-grow root crop.

2. Tomatoes (*Lycopersicon esculentum*), which may grow to 1.5 m (5 ft), require staking.

3. Marigolds (*Tagetes*) are colourful annuals growing to 50 cm (1 ft 8 in).

4. Chives (*Allium schoenoprasum*) form a clump about 30 cm (1 ft) across.

5. Parsley (*Petroselinum crispum*) is an annual herb growing to 30 cm (1 ft).

6. Basil (*Ocimum basilicum*) is a leafy annual herb growing to 75 cm (2½ ft).

# The Traditional Garden

This neat, well-ordered kitchen garden is the one most commonly seen illustrated in gardening books, and the one most time-consuming to maintain. A successful traditional vegetable garden can be the full-time hobby of a retired person, or can be a communal effort requiring several hours of shared work every week. Well-maintained, this style of vegetable plot will greatly add to the charm of your garden. Carefully tended rows of healthy crops provide a constant supply of fresh, nutritious vegetables, herbs and fruits.

The traditional garden can be large or small, depending on the space available. It is most commonly located at the back or side of the house, the position depending on where the most sun is available. Beds are often raised above ground level to provide better drainage and to allow for the additional layers of organic matter, such as well rotted manures or composts, that are used as a mulch between rows and around plants.

Weeds are the main enemy of the traditional garden, invading the space between plants and competing for moisture and nutrients. As plants are organised in rows, with room between them for the gardener to walk, it is only natural that all sorts of weeds will self-sow

*ABOVE: A small-scale traditional garden with timber edges and woodchip pathways for easy access. A small fence keeps animals out of the garden.*
*OPPOSITE: Orderliness is a keynote of traditional vegetable gardening, with seedlings arranged in neat rows and spaces left between them for routine maintenance such as weeding and feeding.*

## *The Traditional Garden*

*F*eatures such as carefully espaliered fruiting trees can make a traditional vegetable garden quite labour-intensive, demanding routine weeding, feeding and general maintenance. This large, productive garden is capable of feeding an entire family, with plenty left over for freezing or preserving. Backed by a high stone wall, this garden will experience additional warmth which will allow for an extended growing period for favourite crops. In all but the coldest climates many varieties will be grown year round, while others will be cultivated routinely on a seasonal basis.

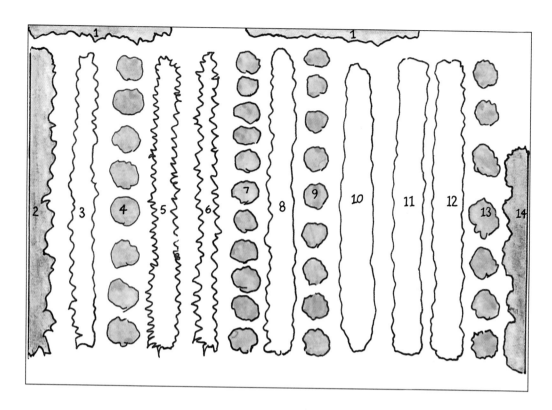

## Key to planting scheme

1. Apple trees (*Malus pumila*) trained against a sunny wall, produce a crop in autumn.
2. Sweet corn (*Zea mays*) positioned so as not to cast shade on smaller species.
3. Beetroot (*Beta vulgaris*) is a root crop that is not particularly demanding.
4. Cabbage (*Brassica oleracea* var. *capitata*) is a heavy feeder, and should be followed by a root crop.
5. Carrot (*Daucus carota*) must be thinned when seedlings are 10 cm (4 in) tall.
6. Onion (*Allium cepa*) is an easy-to-grow root crop.
7. Cauliflower (*Brassica oleracea* var. *botrytis*) is a very heavy feeder demanding rich soil conditions and frequent fertilising.

8. Spinach (*Spinacia oleracea*) produces vitamin-rich crops and needs only minimum ground space.
9. Lettuce (*Lactuca sativa*) has varieties that can be grown year round in all but the coldest climates.
10. Potatoes (*Solanum tuberosum*) are useful for breaking up the ground for other root crops.
11. Dwarf beans (*Phaseolus vulgaris*) demand soil that has been limed prior to planting.
12. Broad beans (*Vica faba*) are a hardy crop for the cooler weather.
13. Tomatoes (*Lycopersicon esculentum*) must have lateral growths removed as they grow.
14. Runner beans (*Phaseolus coccineus*) need the support of a fence or trellis. Add lime to the ground prior to planting.

and spring up, spoiling the appearance and productivity of the garden. This is where a thick mulch layer is especially valuable; even straw or newspapers can be used to suppress rampant invasion of weeds.

In our traditional garden plan, a wall surrounding the garden provides protection, and creates a warm micro-climate, even in cool to cold climates. The wall is also used to support trellises for growing a variety of climbing crops or vines on, and forms a warm backdrop against which fruiting varieties have been espaliered. A narrow pathway allows easy access to these for general maintenance, pruning and, of course, harvesting.

The neat rows of vegetables have been arranged so that heavy-feeding crops are located next to less demanding varieties, but are not competing with them. Note that plants have been positioned rather close together. To produce good results, this intensive growing method requires a very rich and fertile soil indeed, and frequent feeding and watering.

Routine hoeing between rows is required to prevent the soil surface from becoming compacted, and to allow good air circulation. Compaction can be reduced by mulching with organic matter.

As a general rule taller-growing plants should be located at the back of the garden, where they won't prevent valuable sunlight from reaching smaller species. Separate beds should be provided for perennial varieties such as artichokes, asparagus, strawberries and rhubarb. Invasive vine crops such as pumpkins and squash, and those needing plenty of space, such as potatoes, have been located separately.

# The Potager Garden

This delightful, stylised method of growing vegetables comes to us from France, where the most famous example is the wonderful potager garden at the Chateau Villandry in the Loire Valley.

The concept of a potager garden is to combine vegetables and flowers in decorative patterns, breaking away from the standard design of straight rows. Some people have described this garden style as a triumph of art over craft, since it employs symmetry and use of foliage colours and textures to achieve its creative effect.

Vegetables are grouped together in a sumptuous display, and the effect, when viewed from above, resembles a colourful tapestry. Although there is no limit to individual creativity, most designers of potager gardens choose the more tidy and decorative vegetables for the display, avoiding rambling or climbing crops such as pumpkins or squash.

The original potager garden at Villandry is the culmination of two very strong French traditions—love of food and love of strict geometric artistic patterns—*le potager en parterre*. This garden is edged in traditional English box, and the rows between beds are covered with a light beige gravel.

One of the secrets of the success of a potager is in the arrangement of the various vegetables. The width and height of each species is as important as the foliage colour and texture, and plants are positioned according to their size, with the lower growing species at the front of the garden. Certain flowering annuals are sometimes incorporated into the planting scheme, to add colour and interest. Consider using edible flowers such as nasturtiums, violas or angelica for this purpose.

Taller vegetables for the back of the garden can include broad beans, broccoli, cauliflower, eggplant, rhubarb (a perennial), silverbeet (Swiss chard), spinach, tomatoes or peas, and beans (trained onto a trellis). Smaller-growing species suited to the middle or front of the garden include basil, dwarf beans, beetroot (beets), carrots, celery, chives, cabbage, parsley, onions, radish, bush tomatoes or turnips.

This basic concept can be adapted in any garden, and the shape of the beds can be varied according to personal preference. Almost any vegetables or herbs can be incorporated into the scheme. Remember though, that the symmetry will be spoilt as the crops are harvested! But remember too that these are gardens for picking and enjoying, not just for gazing on and admiring!

*LEFT: Vegetables and herbs carefully arranged according to size, foliage colour and texture in a potager scene. Eventually, despite their beauty in the garden, they will have to be harvested!*

# *The Potager Garden*

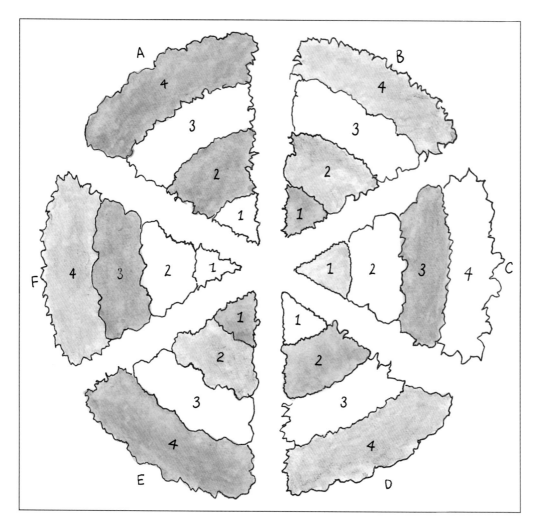

This stylised layout is based on a circle divided into six equal segments. Within each segment, rows of vegetables, herbs and annuals have been arranged according to their size, foliage colour and texture. A great deal of time and effort has gone into making the mature garden a thing of beauty. Colour has been introduced for visual effect using popular long-flowering annuals.

*FOLLOWING PAGE: The appearance of the garden will vary seasonally according to which vegetables, herbs and flowers are mature. Annuals add a splash of colour, and some also have edible flowers or foliage.*

### *Key to planting scheme*

Bed A
1. Camomile (*Matricaria chamomilla*) 45 cm (1½ ft).
2. Carrots (*Daucus carota*) 30 cm (1 ft).
3. Spinach (*Spinacia oleracea*) 60 cm (2 ft).
4. Brussel sprouts (*Brassica oleracea* var. *bullata gemifera*) 1.2 m (4 ft).

Bed B
1. Ageratum (*Ageratum houstonianum*) 45 cm (1½ ft).
2. Chervil (*Anthriscus cerefolium*) 45 cm (1½ ft) and lettuce (*Lactuca sativa*) 30 cm (1 ft).
3. Broccoli (*Brassica oleracea* var. *italica*) 45 cm (1½ ft).
4. Garlic (*Allium sativum*) 1.4 m (5 ft) and dill (*Anethum graveolens*) 90 cm (3 ft).

Bed C
1. Thyme (*Thymus vulgaris*) 15 cm (6 in).
2. Lettuce (*Lactuca sativa*) 30 cm (1 ft).
3. Potatoes (*Solanum tuberosum*) 60 cm (2 ft).
4. Sweet corn (*Zea mays*) 2 m (6 ft).

Bed D
1. Lobelia (*Lobelia erinus*) 20 cm (8 in).
2. Parsley (*Petroselinum crispum*) 30 cm (1 ft) and beetroot (*Beta vulgaris*) 45 cm (1½ ft).
3. Leeks (*Allium ampeloprasum*) and onions (*Allium cepa*) 60 cm (2 ft).
4. Tomatoes (*Lycopersicon esculentum*) 1.4 m (5 ft).

Bed E
1. Nasturtiums (*Tropaeolum*) 30 cm (1 ft).
2. Endive (*Chicorium endivia*) 45 cm (1½ ft) and oregano (*Origanum vulgare*) 60 cm (2 ft).
3. Cauliflower (*Brassica oleracea* var. *botrytis*) 60 cm (2 ft).
4. Broad beans (*Vica faba*) 1.2 m (4 ft).

Bed F
1. Viola (*Viola hybrida*) 20 cm (8 in).
2. Chickory (*Cichorium intybus*) 30 cm (1 ft) and mint (*Mentha*) 45 cm (1½ ft).
3. Cabbage (*Brassica oleracea* var. *capitata*) 60 cm (2 ft).
4. French beans (*Phaseolus vulgaris*) 60 cm (2 ft).

# *The Herb Garden*

Those with space will enjoy creating a separate herb garden, preferably located somewhere near the kitchen. All herb gardens require warm, sheltered conditions and well drained soil, so this environment must be provided if the plants are to produce good results.

As in all gardens, if you want to produce a soft and pleasant effect, avoid planting in straight lines and rigid rows. Herbs are such interesting plants that they can be used as a landscaper would use perennials in a herbaceous border. Many herbs have wonderful foliage and flowers, plus a strong fragrance that makes them perfect for locating near a verandah, patio or other outdoor living area, so that their fragrance can be enjoyed.

This garden plan uses a wide range of annual and perennial herbs, most of them commonly available. A small path through the garden allows easy access for weeding and harvesting, while the curved wall at the back of the garden acts as a sun and warmth trap to improve growing conditions.

Remember that many herbs are clump-forming and will spread, so allow sufficient space around them for adequate growth. Obviously the lower growing varieties are best located at the front of the garden where they can get plenty of sun, with the taller species used as a backdrop.

Herbs are generally quite pest- and disease-resistant, but when young are subject to attack by snails and slugs. They should be picked routinely, and either used fresh, or dried in bunches and stored for later use.

In winter when the garden is dormant, well rotted organic matter can be used to cover the bed in readiness for the following season. Most perennial herbs die back completely in moderate to cold climates, their root systems remaining under the ground. Mulching not only provides a much needed nutritional boost, but also protects them from frosts in really cold areas. Annual herbs also disappear in winter, although many varieties will self-sow, and pop up again in spring when the ground becomes warm.

*LEFT: Make a feature of the herb garden, perhaps as the centrepiece of a formal ornamental garden, or as a surround to a small statue, fountain or pond.*

*FOLLOWING PAGE: Herbs must have plenty of sun and a light, well drained soil to produce good results. Where space permits they can be interplanted with annuals, bulbs and other perennials.*

## *The Herb Garden*

An open, sunny location and light, well drained soil are the requirements for the successful herb garden. Use curved lines in the garden and avoid straight-edged beds. Combine herbs according to height, foliage colour and texture, and put in a pathway to ensure easy access for harvesting. Although many herb species originated in the Mediterranean regions they can be grown in a wide range of climates if the right growing conditions are provided. Frequent picking helps to encourage new growth and prevents annual varieties from running to seed early in the season.

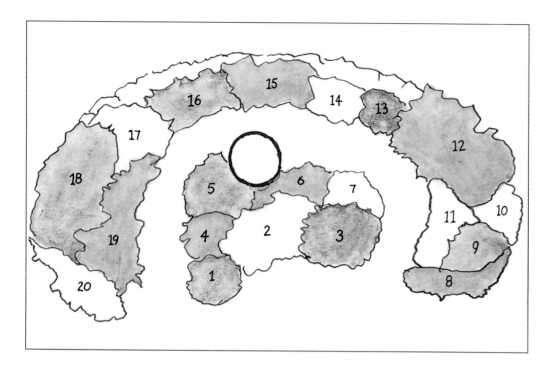

## Key to planting scheme

1. Horseradish (*Cochlearis armoracia*) 30 cm (1 ft)
2. Parsley (*Petroselinum crispum*) 30 cm (1 ft)
3. Chives (*Allium schoenoprasum*) 30 cm (1 ft)
4. Chervil (*Anthriscus cerefolium*) 45 cm (1½ ft)
5. Rosemary (*Rosmarinus officinalis*) 1.5 m (5 ft)
6. Tarragon (*Artemisia dracunculus*) 90 cm (3 ft)
7. Oregano (*Origanum vulgare*) 60 cm (2 ft)
8. Thyme (*Thymus*) 15 cm (6 in)
9. Mint (*Mentha*) 45 cm (1½ ft)
10. Apple mint (*Mentha*) 45 cm (1½ ft)
12. Fennel (*Foemiculum vulgare*) 90 cm (3 ft)
13. Lemon grass (*Cymbopogon citratus*) 1.5 m (5 ft)
14. Garlic (*Allium sativum*) 1.4 m (5 ft)
15. Comfrey (*Symphytum officinalis*) 1.2 m (4 ft)
16. Sage (*Salvia officinalis*) 90 cm (3 ft)
17. Coriander (*Coriandrum sativum*) 60 cm (2 ft)
18. Dill (*Anethum graveolens*) 90 cm (3 ft)
19. Nasturtium (*Tropaeolum*) 30 cm (1 ft)
20. Camomile (*Matricaria chamomilla*) 45 cm (1½ ft)

# PREPARING THE WAY

# The Soil

To ensure the productivity of the vegetable garden, first invest some time in the preparation of the soil. The garden can only be as good as the ground in which it is growing, so energy spent preparing the way will certainly pay off at harvesting time.

There are various aspects of soil management that should be understood by the home gardener. To be fertile, soil must not only contain the right balance of nutrients and minerals, but it must also be of a certain texture to make those nutrients and minerals available to the plants.

## SOIL TEXTURE

Soil can be generally divided into three main categories according to its texture: clay soil, average loam or sandy soil.

Clay soil is dense, heavy and hard to cultivate. The basic factor distinguishing this soil type is the lack of air particles to ventilate and move nutrients through the

*OPPOSITE: Intensive growing conditions demand rich soil, with plenty of organic matter dug in or used as a surface mulch to ensure a light, friable texture.*

*PREVIOUS PAGE: Healthy, disease-free carrot tops. Before establishing a vegetable garden basic groundwork must be done to ensure optimum growing conditions.*

soil. To recognise this soil type perform a simple 'thread test'. This involves mixing a small handful of soil with water, and rolling it between your hands to form a sausage shape. If the mixture forms a smooth, slippery shape that can be bent easily without crumbling, it is considered to be heavy in texture and therefore requires the addition of plenty of organic matter to lift and aerate the soil.

Average loam is neither too heavy nor too light in texture. When you perform the 'thread test' it will form a neat sausage shape that can be bent a little, but will eventually crumble when bent too far. Average loam is ideal for the home vegetable garden, although it will probably still require the addition of some organic matter to boost nutrients and keep it friable.

Sandy soil contains a high proportion of sand and lacks sufficient organic matter to hold soil moisture. The problem with this type of soil is that it dries out too quickly after rainfall or watering, and therefore the plants simply cannot absorb nutrients and minerals contained within the soil. When performing the 'thread test' you will find it difficult to form sandy soil into a sausage shape, and it will certainly crumble apart when it is bent. To correct the texture of sandy or light soil, again the addition of organic matter will create the right balance.

## WHAT IS ORGANIC MATTER?

In gardening, the term 'organic matter' is constantly used. It refers to a wide range of natural materials such as animal manures and composts that are used to enrich the soil and improve its texture. Soil that is constantly used for production will eventually become depleted unless additional organic matter is incorporated to replenish and revitalise the ground. Constant watering, wind, harsh sun and the demands of various crops will rapidly reduce the fertility of the soil, and unless careful steps are taken to keep up with these environmental demands, the garden cannot sustain viable production.

## ANIMAL MANURES

Farmers and gardeners have always made use of animal waste to enrich their soils. In semi-rural areas these materials are readily available, and in cities they can be bought in dried or granulated form by the bag or delivered by a nursery or landscape supplier. Rose growers swear that horse manure is the most effective mulch for their garden beds, while vegetable gardeners prefer poultry manure because it is high in nitrogen, a constantly required nutrient for the production of leafy crops. Sheep and cow manure are also frequently used as soil additives,

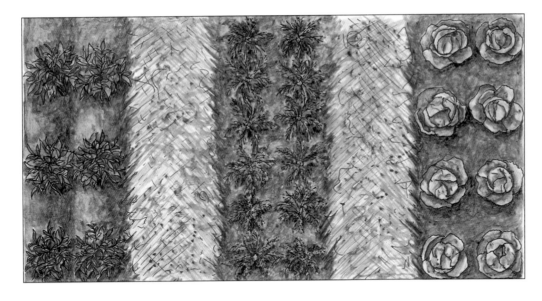

*ABOVE: Compost can be manufactured in rows between plants by layering organic ingredients and covering them with straw. After the crops have been harvested, dig in the compost and use this area for planting a fresh crop.*

*RIGHT: Two practical methods: the compost tumbler provides excellent air penetration when the ingredients are rotated, while the ground-level bin keeps the compost tidy yet allows direct contact with the soil surface.*

mulch or ingredients for the compost.

Care must be taken when using manures to prevent fresh or unrotted manure coming into direct contact with plants, especially plant root systems. Manures should first be seasoned, either by being allowed to rot in a pile mixed with straw or grass clippings, or by being added to the compost heap where they will create heat and hasten decomposition of the other organic matter.

## COMPOST

The other useful organic additive is compost. Compost is decomposed vegetable matter that has broken down to form a rich, light and friable humus. A well balanced garden will contain a rich resource of organic materials for composting, and eventually the garden should become self-sufficient, creating enough compost to constantly regenerate the soil.

By composting, nothing in the garden (or the house) is wasted. An efficient compost heap is made by layering these organic materials in heaps where they become hot and eventually decompose.

Compost needs moisture and air to decompose. A compost heap should be watered once a week if there is no rainfall, and lightly turned over every few weeks with a fork to encourage air to travel through the heap.

The smaller the size of the ingredi-

| NUTRIENT PERCENTAGE IN DIFFERENT MANURES | | | |
| --- | --- | --- | --- |
| Manure | nitrogen | phosphorus | potassium |
| Cow | 1.0 | 0.4 | 0.5 |
| Poultry | 2.1 | 1.6 | 1.0 |
| Poultry pellets | 5.0 | 3.3 | 1.5 |
| Horse | 0.7 | 0.4 | 0.5 |
| Pig | 1.1 | 0.7 | 0.1 |
| Sheep | 1.8 | 0.4 | 0.5 |

ents, the faster the decomposition. Grass clippings, for example, become hot very quickly, and assist the rapid breaking down of the other materials. Large leaves, stems, twigs or bark will slow down the process unless they are cut up or shredded in a composting (shredding) machine. The concept is to combine as many ingredients as possible, and let the heap rot over a period of eight to ten weeks.

The heap can be made directly on the ground where the compost is to be used, and this indeed is a great way of preparing a new bed for planting. Instead of making the compost in one particular location, then moving it by barrow to where it is to be spread, consider composting an area of lawn, then turning it over ready for planting after a few months! Some vegetable gardeners use this method within the vegetable patch, by clearing away one crop and composting the left-over stalks, roots or outside leaves together with straw, grass clippings and manure, creating a fallow bed for the following season. This method works well because it gives the strip of ground a chance to rest, while increasing organic matter and earthworm numbers in preparation for a fresh crop.

## Compost ingredients
- animal manures
- straw or hay
- grass clippings
- leaves
- shredded stalks and bark
- kitchen vegetable scraps
- floor sweepings/contents of vacuum cleaner bag
- seaweed
- mushroom compost
- shredded newspaper
- weeds
- sawdust or wood shavings

All of these organic ingredients will break down if small enough in size, and providing the heap is kept hot and active. By making compost directly on the ground rather than in a container, earthworms can travel upwards and circulate through the heap, which also helps to move things along more rapidly.

There are certain plants, such as legumes or comfrey, that are also good activators for compost. Shred their leaves and roots, add them to the heap, and the entire process will take less time!

## PREPARING A FIRST-TIME GARDEN

Converting an area of lawn or garden wilderness into a productive vegetable garden can be a daunting task, although there are many shortcuts to success.

A site must first be cleared of all large debris, such as stones, rocks or gravel. Avoid digging too deeply into the ground and disturbing the natural structure of the soil unless there is a tremendous need for the addition of organic matter in the form of manures or compost. Even so these additives are best added in layers on the soil surface and allowed to mulch down into the soil, rather than dug in at any depth.

To remove grass or weeds from the soil surface simply lift them in sections, then either remove them completely from the site to be composted, or turn them over with their roots facing upwards to be killed by the sun. Afterwards they can be lightly incorporated back into the soil. Allow a bit of time to prepare the bed for the first planting. Digging over the soil and removing grass and weeds can be done in autumn, then a layer of fresh manure can be added and the bed left to settle during winter, ready for your first spring planting.

An easy and fast way of preparing the first-time garden is to cover the soil surface with layers of newspaper, manure and straw, immediately suppressing grass and weeds. This is often known as the no-

*Concrete or brick stepping stones between rows allow easy access for planting, weeding and harvesting. A timber tepee will support a second crop of climbing beans* (Phaseolus coccineus).

dig method, because little or no cultivation of the soil is required. As the straw and manure break down they provide an instant growing environment for a wide range of crops. Root crops such as potatoes can be planted beneath the newspaper layer, with some area left open for them to emerge. This provides the double benefit of breaking down the soil underneath, aerating it and encouraging earthworms. The following season a leaf crop may be planted in an area where only six months previously there was lawn!

No matter which method is employed, ensure that the garden is adequate for the family needs. It may be best to start with a moderate-size bed, then add to it as you become more confident, remembering that a large garden will require many hours of maintenance. Consider creating separate beds for perennial crops such as rhubarb, asparagus or artichokes.

# *Planting Plans*

Planting the garden in a haphazard fashion will rarely give good results. Even a permaculture garden requires careful planning and designing in the initial stages, to produce the required results.

By designing the layout of the garden to incorporate crop rotation, succession planting and companion planting, the harvest will be greatly enhanced.

## COMPANION PLANTING

This method has been practised by successful gardeners for centuries, and is based on the knowledge that certain plants grow well together, and in some cases actually have a positive effect on the health of their companions. The reasons for this simpatico are not as mysterious as they may seem. Tall-growing plants, for example, can provide shelter and protection for species that are smaller and more vulnerable. Low-growing plants are often of benefit to their neighbours by providing shade and wind protection for their roots. This is why pumpkins and other vine crops are often planted in and around a patch of corn which is susceptible

*RIGHT: Careful planning and design of the garden to incorporate crop rotation, succession planting and companion planting will ensure a healthy, disease-free harvest.*

| TYPICAL COMPANION PLANTS | |
|---|---|
| **Herb** | **Companion** |
| Basil | Grows well with tomatoes; repels flies and mosquitoes |
| Borage | Grows well with tomatoes, squash and strawberries; repels tomato worm |
| Camomile | Grows well with cabbage and onions |
| Chervil | Grows well with radish |
| Chives | Grows well with carrots |
| Dill | Grows well with cabbage; avoid planting near carrots |
| Garlic | Grows well near raspberries; repels Japanese beetle |
| Horseradish | Grows well near potatoes; repels potato bug |
| Marigolds | Excellent repellent of nematodes, beetles and other insects |
| Mint | Grows well with cabbage; repels white cabbage moth |
| Nasturtium | Grows well with cabbage, radishes, cucurbits; repels aphids, pumpkin beetles |
| Rosemary | Grows well with cabbage, beans and carrots; repels cabbage moth, carrot fly |
| Thyme | Grows well with all brassicas; repels cabbage worm |

Instead of locating them in a section of their own, they can be incorporated throughout the beds to improve the growth, health and flavour of a wide range of species. Some herbs exude aromatic oils that repel insects, while others attract insects and therefore keep them away from the crops.

## SUCCESSION PLANTING

A well organised vegetable garden will be planned to allow space for routine planting of various staple crops such as lettuce, cabbage, spinach and beans.

The theory behind this method is quite simple. Instead of planting thirty or forty lettuce and having them all ready for harvesting at once, small quantities are planted in succession, keeping a steady supply of fresh vegetables ready for harvesting over many months. Therefore six lettuce are planted in one section of the garden, and two weeks later another six are planted.

The success of succession planting will depend on the climate. In tropical and temperate regions it is possible to have successive crops of certain species going all year round, providing they are not ready for harvesting mid-summer, when there is a danger of their 'bolting to seed'. That is, flowering before there is time to harvest them. In cool to cold climates the growing season is limited by the weather conditions, with many crops unsuitable for growing in autumn or winter. These climates, however, are ideal for a wide range of 'winter crops' such as brussels sprouts and broccoli, that may

*Strawberries (*Fragaria*) and tomatoes (*Lycopersicon esculentum*) benefit from close proximity, while in the background sweet corn (*Zea* mays) can be underplanted with pumpkin (*Cucurbita maxima*) for mutually good results.*

to the drying out of the soil surface. The large canopy of pumpkin leaves actually performs as a natural mulch, helping to keep the ground cool and moist.

Some plants, such as marigolds and nasturtiums, exude an aroma that helps to repel insects which means other nearby species are safe from attack. Root crops and leaf crops grow well side-by-side because they are not competing for the same ground space or nutrients. Likewise positioning plants with deep and strong

root systems near root crops is also beneficial because the deep roots will break up hard soils, making it much easier for the root crops to penetrate the soil.

Certain plants have the ability to concentrate or collect high concentrations of certain elements, which can then become available to other plants. Sometimes these plants can be dug back into the soil to boost the general nutrient level.

Herbs are effectively used as companion plants for the vegetable garden.

*Space has been left between rows to allow for the planting of successive crops. As one crop is harvested, the ground is prepared for subsequent planting.*

not do so well in the warmer districts.

Modern hybridisation of seeds has also resulted in varieties that can be grown winter and summer, planted in succession.

This manner of planting is economical if plants are grown from seed, because a small number can be germinated at one time ready for planting out when they are of a reasonable size. Buying seedlings means only that twelve to fifteen plants will be ready at one time, which is too many in summer when mature plants last only a short time in the ground.

## CROP ROTATION

This age-old practice helps preserve the soil, preventing it from becoming depleted by over-use. Crop rotation means that no two species or groups of plants (i.e. brassicas, cucurbits) are grown in the one area of the garden in successive seasons. It can also mean that certain parts of the garden are allowed to lie fallow, without supporting a crop, to regenerate and be ready for the following season.

In general, a heavy feeding leaf crop such as cabbage or lettuce should be fol-lowed by a less demanding root crop such as carrots or turnips. Root crops often resent soils that have been recently enriched with manures or fertilisers, and thrive in soils that have been manured the previous season for a demanding crop.

When planning a garden using crop rotation principles, it is best to draw a simple garden plan on paper and mark out where each variety is planted, and the date. This way it is possible to keep track of where each group of plants is located, so that a complementary crop can be planted in that space the following season.

# Methods & Maintenance

The most enjoyable aspects of vegetable gardening must surely be first the planting and then the harvesting—the planting because it holds such a promise of things to come; the harvesting because it is the reward for all that hard work and patience.

After planning and designing the layout of the garden and preparing the soil, it is time to plant out the first crops. Spring is the best time for starting a first-time garden, because the coming warm growing season will bring encouraging results. In cooler climates ensure that the ground is warm and the danger of frost has passed, especially for more tender crops like tomatoes.

## SEEDS
The most economical method of growing vegetables is raising them from seed either sown directly in the ground where the plants are to grow, or raised to seedling stage in trays or punnets (cell packs). Apart from the cost saving, seeds are also preferable because the gardener can control just how many are to be germinated at one time, which assists with succession planting of various crops.

There is plenty of scope and choice in seed selection. Commercial seed companies produce a wide range of modern

*Seedlings raised in trays can be transplanted when large enough to handle easily. This should be done in the early evening when the sun has left the garden.*

hybridised vegetable seeds, many of which have been chemically treated against fungal disease before being packaged. Newer organic seed producers have also made widely available a range of old-fashioned 'nostalgia' vegetable seedlings, which are useful for gardeners who wish to gather their own seed from their crops at the end of each season.

Hybridised plants do not usually produce viable seeds, and although they have been developed to resist certain diseases, some gardeners prefer the old varieties,

claiming they are tougher, more diverse and more interesting than their modern counterparts.

## SOWING FROM SEED
In general, when sowing seeds, follow the instructions on the packet about the particular requirements of each species.

Seeds need a warm, moist environment to germinate successfully, and there are various ways of ensuring this environment to increase the success rate of the germination.

Seeds sown in trays or punnets (cell packs) must be bedded in a light but fertile propagation mixture, which can be bought commercially or mixed using sand, compost and peat. This growing medium needs to be light but capable of holding moisture, to help the seeds sprout. There are various commercially available organic growing-pots, in which seeds can be raised and which then can be planted directly in the garden without needing to disturb their root systems. These pots are good, although they do add to the cost of establishing each plant.

Most seeds should be planted at a depth that is in proportion to their size, i.e. the larger the seed, the deeper it needs to be planted. Tiny seeds, like those of the carrot, are difficult to sow because of their size. They are generally mixed with sand and scattered in shallow drills, topped with a sprinkling of soil then pressed down lightly. After germination the seeds will still require thinning out, so that there are spaces between those remaining in the drill. Larger seeds, such as corn or beans, are easier to handle and can be spaced out as required.

When sowing seed directly in the ground where plants are to grow, the soil must be kept lightly moist until germination is successful. In hot conditions a hessian sack may be used to prevent the soil surface from drying out during the heat of the day. In cool conditions a sheet of clear plastic over the soil surface will trap the warmth and help hasten germination.

Seeds grown directly in the ground are often stronger because they do not suffer the setback experienced during transplanting from seedbox to the garden. Wherever possible try growing directly from seed, ensuring that the emerging seedlings are protected from snails and slugs.

## GATHERING SEED

It is possible to gather your own seed by allowing one plant in each crop to flower and 'run to seed' every season. This will generally only work with non-hybridised plants, although some of these varieties will reproduce a replica of one of the parent plants.

Choose a healthy, strong-growing plant to ensure the most robust seed is produced. The seeds must be mature before being harvested, and this occurs naturally if the plant is allowed to turn

*Geraniums (*Pelargonium*), nasturtiums (*Tropaeolum*) and marigolds (*Tagetes*) happily co-exist with a rambling pumpkin vine (*Cucurbita*) in a mixed bed, built above ground level to improve drainage.*

brown—in fact it should be nearly dead before the seeds are gathered. Store sufficient for the following season in a paper envelope, marked with variety and date, and keep this in a dark, dry place. If there are still seeds left on the plant collect them and scatter them throughout the garden. Many will germinate where they fall, and can be later transplanted (although in permaculture they are allowed to grow wherever they self-sow!)

Some gardeners have a small area set aside as a 'seed bank' where they grow one example of each crop just for the purpose of setting seed. In this plot the seeds are either harvested and stored for the following season, or allowed to self-sow and germinate naturally, before being transplanted into the main garden.

## TRANSPLANTING SEEDLINGS

Care should be taken during the transplanting process to ensure that seedlings do not suffer a setback or trauma. Healthy young plants should be approximately 10 cm (4 in) in height and quite robust before transplanting, either from seed trays, punnets (cell packs) or another part of the garden. Early evening is the best time to transplant, when the sun has gone from the garden; and both the potting mixture in the seed trays and the soil where they are to be planted should be lightly damp. When handling seedlings take care not to damage their stems or delicate root systems—never allow them to be exposed to the sun or to dry out. After transplanting, water the ground lightly and provide some protection from snails and slugs. During hot weather also provide some temporary sun protection—a shade cloth covering is ideal. When plants have become established and start to grow they should be mulched, but avoid mulching against the stems of the plants, which can cause fungal disease.

## WEEDING

Weeds compete with vegetables for moisture, nutrients and space. Although some organic gardeners allow weeds to intermingle with crops as companion plants, they have no place in the traditional kitchen garden. Prevention is a better strategy than trying to cope with weeds once they have gained a stranglehold.

Gardens that are mulched with grass clippings, newspaper or straw succeed in keeping weed infestation under control. Once the ground has been cleared and the young seedlings are established, a thick layer of mulch should be applied to suppress weed growth between rows and between individual plants.

When removing weeds always catch them in the early stages, before they have a chance to seed and spread. Weeds can be incorporated into a compost heap, providing it is good and hot, as their seeds will be destroyed. (A slow burning compost invariably has a variety of self-sown seedlings sprouting from it.)

Weeding moist ground is easier and more effective than trying to remove weeds from dry, hard-packed soil. Water the ground thoroughly the day before weeding, and ensure that the whole of the plant, including the root system is removed. Weeds can also be destroyed by pulling them up and exposing their roots to the sun. They can then be composted safely.

## MULCHING

Effective mulching is probably the most vital step to successful vegetable cultivation. A layer of mulch covering the surface between plants will help to keep the soil moist and prevent the surface from drying out, even in hot windy conditions. The mulch layer will also keep weed growth down and, if organic mulches are used, it will provide a steady stream of nutrients to growing plants.

To be effective a mulch layer should be at least 2.5 cm (1 in) deep. Mulch can be applied in various layers, i.e. a thin layer of manure or compost topped by grass clippings, straw or newspaper. The manure layer will provide nutrients, and the straw, grass clippings or newspaper will suppress weeds.

Useful mulches include:
- all animal manures after they have been rotted
- compost
- straw
- grass clippings
- leaves
- bark
- newspaper and cardboard.

Avoid inorganic mulches such as plastic, which can overheat the soil and prevent natural air circulation. Always allow a space around the base of plants to allow air movement. If a deep mulch layer is pressing against plant stems, it can result in too much humidity and therefore fungal problems.

In a fertile vegetable garden, layers of mulch are constantly added, improving the soil texture and fertility. As one layer breaks down into the soil, another is added to provide continuing protection.

## WATERING

Most vegetable gardens, even in climates where there is a high rainfall, will require some additional water. During summer, hot winds and high temperatures can dry out the soil surface, and regular watering becomes a necessity.

In warmer seasons, always water during the early morning or in the evening, never in the heat of the day. In winter avoid evening waterings because moisture drops can freeze overnight destroying foliage. It is better to water thoroughly every few days than to give plants a light watering every day. Daily light watering will encourage plant roots to grow upwards in search of moisture, while deep watering will help plants to become more deep-rooted, and therefore stronger.

As mentioned previously, a good layer of mulch will help prevent the soil from drying out and reduce the amount of watering that is required.

Some plants, such as tomatoes, prefer to be watered at ground level. A system of soaker hoses that release small quanti-

*Straw is a useful mulching material, especially when organic matter such as manure or compost has been layered underneath to feed plants as they grow.*

ties of water directly into the ground rather than spraying water overhead are useful in this situation.

Watering by hand affords an excellent opportunity of checking on the health of the garden. While watering, inspect plants, looking at the back of their leaves for sign of disease or pest infestation.

## FEEDING

The amount of feeding required will depend on the original fertility of the soil and the individual vegetable variety. Some species are heavy feeders and require a constant supply of nutrients to keep them growing rapidly. Other species resent soil that is over-fertilised, and

require no plant food after sowing.

Organic fertilisers are slower to act than chemical plant foods, but in the long term they are better for the health of the garden. Building up the soil and its structure with well-rotted manures and compost will create an excellent growing environment, and plants may only require an occasional side-dressing of organic fertiliser to crop well.

## LIQUID PLANT FOOD

This is an effective way of feeding growing plants, as the liquid is rapidly absorbed by the roots. Organic and chemical liquid plant foods are commercially available, and they can be diluted

and either watered into the ground around plants or sprayed onto the leaves.

Homemade liquid fertiliser can be produced by mixing seaweed or fresh animal manure with water in a large drum or plastic garbage bin. After several weeks the resulting smelly liquid can be diluted with three parts of water. If poultry manure is the base, the liquid will be high in nitrogen and useful for leafy green crops.

## DRY FERTILISER

Powdered or granulated fertilisers are popular and they can be incorporated at planting time, or later lightly dug into the ground around plants as a side-dressing. Look for specially formulated mixtures designed to feed individual crops such as tomatoes or leaf crops, which require a fertiliser high in nitrogen. Try to feed each group of plants according to need. Crops such as celery, for example, need to be fed constantly to boost rapid growth. Others, such as carrots, resent over-feeding. Plants grown intensively, closer together than recommended by seed manufacturers, will require more feeding than those given additional space in the garden.

## SLOW RELEASE FERTILISER

Some fertilisers are designed to break down slowly, releasing nutrients to plants at a steady rate over several months. Although these are mostly chemical-based, they certainly benefit the health of the plants by providing a constant source of nutrients.

# The
# BEST
# VEGETABLES

# *Vegetables*

## ARTICHOKE
**Botanical name:** *Cynara scolymus*
**Varieties:** Green Globe and Purple Globe
**Planting:** Grown from suckers taken from an established plant, and planted from autumn to early spring. They should be planted firmly at least 90 cm (3 ft) apart.
**Requirements:** Rich soil and a sunny open position are required, and a climate that is not too humid in summer. As a perennial artichokes can be planted in a separate bed.
**Maintenance:** In summer mulch the plants well with manure or compost, and water routinely. In autumn remove dying stems and leaves and mulch with straw for winter.
**Pests and diseases:** Humid conditions can cause leaf spot.
**Harvesting:** The plump young heads can be cut from spring to summer while the scales are still tight. Use a clean, sharp

*OPPOSITE: Spectacular results can be achieved when plants are well fed. Leafy greens demand plenty of nitrogen-rich fertiliser, which can be applied in liquid form or as a side dressing.*

*PREVIOUS PAGE: Crisp young beans (Phaseolus) are popular with home vegetable gardeners, because they are easy to cultivate.*

*Perennial asparagus (Asparagus officinalis) prefers a climate with cool, crisp winters. Spears can be cut when they reach 10 cm (4 in) in height.*

knife. A healthy plant should last three years or more.

## ASPARAGUS
**Botanical name:** *Asparagus officinalis*
**Varieties:** Mary Washington 500, V.C. 66; select male plants only as they are more productive
**Planting:** Can be grown from seed, but generally one-year-old plants are used because they take less time to grow. Plant them immediately after purchase in late

autumn/early winter, in prepared trenches 25 cm (10 in) deep, 30 cm (1 ft) wide and at least 90 cm (3 ft) apart.
**Requirements:** A cool to cold climate and rich, well drained soil is essential for success. Incorporate plenty of organic matter.
**Maintenance:** In autumn the fern stalks will turn yellow, and should be cut back to ground level. At this stage give the plants a dressing of general fertiliser, then mound up the soil around them and mulch with well rotted manure.
**Pests and diseases:** Not susceptible, although slugs and snails can be a problem.
**Harvesting:** In the first year no harvesting should be done. From then onwards pick every spring when the asparagus reach 10 cm (4 in) in height. Use a sharp knife to cut the plants at the base. A healthy plant should produce for ten years.

## BEANS
**Botanical name:** *Phaseolus vulgaris* (French beans) *Phaseolus coccineus* (climbing beans)
**Varieties:** Dwarf (Tendergreen, Gourmet's Delight, Canadian Wonder, Brown Beauty, Pioneer, Windsor Long Pod). Climbing (Blue Lake, Epicure, Golden Crop, Scarlet Runner and Scarlet

Emperor, Purple King). Also Snake Beans and Butter Beans.

**Planting:** The first sowing should be in spring, when the danger of frost has passed, as beans will not germinate in cold ground. Second sowings can be made in late summer or autumn, as mid-summer crops tend to fail. Each seed needs to be planted at a depth of 5 cm (2 in), with a distance of 25 cm (10 in) between plants. If planting in rows, make them at least 45 cm (18 in) apart.

**Requirements:** Choose a sunny, open position and rich but well drained soil. Some lime or dolomite should be added prior to planting.

**Maintenance:** Keep the ground well mulched to suppress weed growth, and water well in dry weather. Climbing varieties will need some support such as a trellis, or a fence covered with wire. When flowers are forming a side-dressing of fertiliser will help boost the yield.

**Pests and diseases:** Over-watering after sowing can prevent germination.

**Harvesting:** Dwarf beans crop about ten weeks after sowing; climbing varieties can take slightly longer. Check plants daily, and harvest beans when young and tender, as this will encourage further production.

## BEETROOT (BEETS)

**Botanical name:** *Beta vulgaris*

**Varieties:** Derwent Globe, Early Wonder, Cylindrica, Italian Chioggio, Golden Apollo, Mini Gourmet

**Planting:** Beets are sown from seed from early spring through to late summer, and into autumn in warmer areas. Seeds are

*Broccoli* (Brassica oleracea *var.* italica) *can be grown year round in most climates, but avoid mid-summer harvests which frequently bolt to seed.*

generally sown in drills 2 cm ($^3/_4$ in) deep and 20 cm (8 in) apart.

**Requirements:** Can be grown in a wide range of climates, in soil that is fertile and well drained but not recently manured. Excellent crop to follow a leaf crop such as spinach, lettuce or cabbage.

**Maintenance:** Young plants will need to be thinned out so that they are 15 cm (6 in) apart, and the surrounding ground should be mulched to prevent growth of weeds. Always keep the ground lightly moist (mulch helps with this too). Use a liquid fertiliser every four weeks to keep growth steady.

**Pests and diseases:** Susceptible to 'heart rot' if the soil is deficient in boron.

**Harvesting:** Beets should be harvested and eaten when young and tender, and should be ready after ten weeks from sowing.

## BROCCOLI

**Botanical name:** *Brassica oleracea* var. *italica*

**Varieties:** There are green, white and purple varieties. Also Romanesco, which is an Italian variety.

**Planting:** Can be enjoyed for most of the year, although avoid timing crops to be ready mid-summer, when they will bolt to seed. An excellent winter crop when planted in late summer. Grow from seed or seedlings planted 50 cm (20 in) apart in rows with 60 cm (2 ft) between them.

**Requirements:** Does not require very rich soil and is a good crop to follow peas or beans, where the ground has been heavily manured. Good drainage and an open sunny position is important.

**Maintenance:** Mulch around young plants when they are established, and feed once with a light liquid fertiliser during the growth period. An additional feeding when plants begin to produce will keep the production of new heads going.

**Pests and diseases:** Can suffer fungal diseases in warm, moist soils. Also prone to cabbage moth, cabbage butterfly and aphids.

**Harvesting:** Broccoli can be harvested progressively from about ten to twelve weeks from sowing the seed. Cut the centre head before it flowers, then continue cutting the side heads as they emerge, using a clean, sharp knife.

## BRUSSELS SPROUTS

**Botanical name**: *Brassica oleracea* var. *bullata*

**Varieties:** Jade Cross, Peer Gynt, Top Score, also non-hybrid varieties like Long Island, Yates Champion

**Planting:** As a winter crop sprouts should be sown in mid to late summer. Allow plenty of space, 60–90 cm (2–3 ft), between plants.

**Requirements:** Rich and well drained

*Easy-to-grow cabbage (*Brassica oleracea *var.* capitata*) is available in seed and seedling form in a range of varieties including (clockwise from left) Chinese cabbage, Drumhead, Red cabbage and Savoy. Cabbage can be grown year round in most climates.*

soil is essential, although ground that has been manured for a previous crop is preferable to freshly manured ground. A cool to cold climate is also necessary for success.

**Maintenance:** Mulch around the base of plants to keep the weeds down, and water regularly if conditions are dry. Do not push sprouts ahead with nitrogen-rich fertilisers; instead ensure that the soil is rich prior to planting.

**Pests and diseases**: Like all brassicas, sprouts are prone to attack by white cabbage moths and cabbage butterflies.

**Harvesting:** Sprouts take five to six months to mature. Begin picking them from the base of the main stem, cutting with a sharp knife rather than snapping them off.

## CABBAGE

**Botanical name**: *Brassica oleracea* var. *capitata*

**Varieties:** Many varieties for every growing season including Red cabbage, Drumhead, Sugarloaf, Earliball, Eureka and Green Coronet

**Planting:** Allow a space of about 45 cm (18 in) between plants.

**Requirements:** Like most brassicas, cabbages prefer soil that has been enriched for a previous crop, such as peas or beans. Lime is important, and if none has been added the previous season it should be lightly incorporated at planting time. They are suited for growing most of the year round in all climates, although avoid planting crops to mature in mid-summer, when they will bolt to seed.

**Maintenance:** Protect young seedlings from snails, mulch well and feed once a month with a side-dressing of organic fertiliser.

**Pests and diseases:** Protect from cabbage moths and white cabbage butterflies. Avoid mulching near the stems when young, or stem rot will occur.

**Harvesting:** Pick cabbages when the hearts feel firm and plump. Avoid leaving in the ground too long, or they will become tough. Harvesting times vary according to variety and time of the year.

## CAPSICUM

**Botanical name**: *Capsicum annum*
**Varieties**: Giant Bell (Californian Wonder), Long Red Cayenne, Long Sweet Yellow (Sweet Banana).
**Planting:** Allow a space of 45 cm (18 in) between plants, in rows 60 cm (2 ft) apart. Spring is the usual planting season, except in hot climates when later sowings can be made.
**Requirements:** The soil must be rich and fertile, but not too high in nitrogen which will encourage foliage growth at the expense of fruit production. Dig in

*Root crops resent soils that have been heavily manured or fertilised. They are therefore good crops to follow heavy-feeding ones such as cauliflower and cabbage. Clockwise from left: carrot, parsnip, swede, radish and beetroot.*

well rotted compost before planting. In really cold climates the growing season may be too short, and a glasshouse may be required for successful production.
**Maintenance:** Mulch to keep weeds down, and provide a stake to support the growing plants. Fertilise when the flowers are forming fruit.
**Pests and diseases**: Protect from red spider, leaf mould and mildew.

**Harvesting:** Capsicum need at least 12 weeks to mature, although fruits can be picked sooner for a more bitter taste. Use a clean sharp knife.

## CARROTS

**Botanical name:** *Daucus carota*
**Varieties:** Many varieties for growing all year round, including Western Red, Top Weight, All Seasons, King Chanenay,

Early Horn and Baby Carrot.

**Planting:** The seeds of carrots are very small, making them difficult to sow. They can be sown in shallow drills covered with light soil, or scattered thinly in a well prepared seed bed. Sowings can start in spring, and continue throughout the year except in cool to cold climates where sowing shouldn't extend beyond autumn.

**Requirements:** Carrots need a light, well drained soil, preferably one that has been enriched for a previous crop. Too much manure will produce top growth at the expense of the roots.

**Maintenance:** When seedlings reach 2 cm (³/₄ in) in height, start thinning so that plants are 5 cm (2 in) apart. A later thinning should be done, so that each plant is 10 cm from the next. Keep weeds down and water well in summer.

**Pests and diseases:** Generally disease-free although nematodes can cause deformity of the roots.

**Harvesting:** Young carrots can be harvested progressively, starting with quite small roots. Allow some to grow larger and develop. If left in the ground too long they will split, especially in wet weather.

## CAULIFLOWER

**Botanical name**: *Brassica oleracea* var. *botrytis cauliflora*

**Varieties:** Many varieties with different maturing times including Phenomenal Early, White Knight, Deepheart and Snowball

**Planting:** Can either be grown from seed sown directly in the ground, or raised in seed beds and transplanted when 10 cm (4 in) in height. As they are quite large when mature, a distance of 60 cm (2 ft) will be needed between plants.

**Requirements:** Prefers a cool to cold climate, although can be grown successfully in temperate regions if the right variety is selected. The soil must be rich and well drained, and all-purpose fertiliser added prior to planting.

**Maintenance:** Mulch around plants when established, not too close to the stems, and feed every three weeks with a liquid fertiliser or side-dressing of all-purpose fertiliser. When hearts begin to develop tie the leaves together. This will protect hearts from the sun, which turns them yellow.

**Pests and diseases:** Susceptible to white cabbage butterfly, cabbage moths and aphids. Soil deficiencies (boron, magnesium or molybdenum) will cause failure of crops. Prior to planting, enrich soil well.

**Harvesting:** Allow at least 14–16 weeks for plants to mature. If left in the ground too long they will bolt to seed.

## CELERY

**Botanical name:** *Apium graveolens*

**Varieties:** Many varieties including Crisp Salad and Giant White, American Green and Self-Blanching.

**Planting:** Can be grown from seed planted directly in the ground, although better results are achieved by raising them to seedling stage then transplanting them into the garden. Seedlings should be planted out in spring when danger of frost has passed, and sowings can continue into autumn. Dig a trench prior to planting, and allow a distance of 20 cm (8 in) between seedlings.

**Requirements:** Celery is a heavy feeder and demands rich, fertile and well drained soil. Add plenty of organic matter before planting.

**Maintenance:** To grow quickly, celery demands regular feeding. As the stalks grow they should be protected from sunlight; this is called blanching. They can be wrapped in newspaper and the soil on the sides of the trench mounded up around them.

**Pests and diseases:** Leaf spot is a common problem. Lack of boron in the soil will cause stems to crack.

**Harvesting:** After nine weeks of growth the celery will be ready for harvesting. Dig up plants, harvesting one at a time—or take the outside stalks of the plant, cover the rest and allow the plant to remain in the ground. Do not leave plants too long or they will become tough, bitter and stringy.

## CHICORY

**Botanical name:** *Cichorium intybus*

**Varieties:** Witloof and Long Greenleaf

**Planting:** This plant has an unusual growth pattern, as it is neither the leaf nor the root that is edible, but the blanched chicons which must be grown in darkness. Begin by planting out seeds directly in the ground in drills 1 cm (¹/₂ in) deep and 30 cm (1 ft) apart. In six to eight weeks the roots will be ready for transplanting into a prepared box filled with lightly moist loamy soil. Spring and early summer are the usual sowing times.

**Requirements:** Avoid over-rich soil which can cause forking of the roots.

**Maintenance:** The roots will need to be transplanted into a box, then covered to completely obliterate the light. This box can be kept in a greenhouse or some other sheltered place for four weeks until the chicons have developed.

**Pests and diseases:** Generally trouble-free.

**Harvesting:** Do not harvest until needed as the chicons will quickly become limp when exposed to the light.

## CHINESE CABBAGE

**Botanical name:** *Brassica pekinensis*

**Varieties:** Hybrid Hong Kong, Petsai

**Planting:** Can be grown directly from seed or seedlings, spaced 20 cm (8 in) apart, with a distance of 30 cm (1 ft) between rows.

**Requirements:** Requires rich, moist soil so incorporate plenty of humus before planting. Some shade will be needed if crops are ready for harvesting mid-summer, as this cabbage quickly bolts to seed.

**Maintenance:** Keeping a good supply of water to these plants is essential. Mulch around them to suppress weed growth and water daily. A liquid plant food every three weeks helps maintain rapid growth. The outside leaves can be tied up as the plants begin to heart.

**Pests and diseases:** Not generally a problem.

**Harvesting:** Pick and eat as soon as they are mature which, in the right conditions, can be only eight weeks from sowing. If left in the ground they will flower.

## CUCUMBER

**Botanical name:** *Cucumis sativus*

**Varieties:** Many varieties including Lebanese, apple cucumbers and those for pickling, Paris Pik, Crystal Apple, Green Gem, various Burpless hybrids.

**Planting:** Sow seeds directly where the plants are to grow by cultivating an area 30 cm (1 ft) square and adding plenty of well rotted manure or compost. In the centre make a depression and place several seeds at a depth of 2-3 cm (1-1½ in). Keep moist until germination is successful, and remove the weakest seedlings.

Generally grown as a summer salad crop, with sowings beginning in spring and continuing until mid-summer.

**Requirements:** Rich, moist and well drained soil is essential.

**Maintenance:** To save ground space erect a small trellis to support the climbing vine. Keep weeds down by mulching, water well during hot weather and fertilise regularly to keep growth rapid.

**Pests and diseases:** Protect from snails, slugs, cucumber beetles, squash borers and aphids which carry cucumber mosaic virus.

*Cucumbers* (Cucumis sativus) *need regular watering and feeding to produce plump, crisp fruits. Popular varieties include (clockwise from top) apple cucumber, Lebanese cucumber and green slicing cucumber.*

**Harvesting:** Pick when young and crisp; harvesting times depend on variety, but generally nine to twelve weeks in good conditions. If left too long they will become tough and bitter.

## EGGPLANT

**Botanical name:** *Solanum melongena* var. *esculentum*

**Varieties:** Supreme, Hybrid Mission Bell, Early Long Purple

**Planting:** Best grown to seedling stage and then transplanted into the garden in spring when the soil has warmed and all danger of frost has passed. Plants should be positioned 60 cm (2 ft) apart, in rows about 1 m (3½ ft) apart. In cold climates plants will need to be quite advanced before planting out, as they have a long growing season.

**Requirements:** Must have warm growing conditions. Climates with a long, hot summer give best results. The soil must be rich and well drained, with plenty of organic matter added prior to planting.

**Maintenance:** Staking is necessary to support the plant when in fruit. If large fruits are required limit the quantity to four per plant, removing the rest of the flowers and pinching out the side shoots. Water well in hot weather, and feed routinely to produce good results.

**Pests and diseases:** Trouble free

**Harvesting:** Fruit should be ready for picking after five or six months.

## LEEKS

**Botanical name:** *Allium ampeloprasum*

**Varieties:** Musselburgh is the most commonly grown variety.

*New varieties of lettuce* (Latuca sativa) *are constantly being introduced to satisfy salad-loving consumers. Here shown clockwise from left are butter lettuce, red oakleaf, crisphead and mignonette.*

**Planting:** Can either be raised to seedling stage in trays and then transplanted into the garden, or sown directly in drills and thinned out to a distance of 15 cm (6 in) apart when 15 cm (6 in) tall. Spring and summer are best times to plant.

**Requirements:** Like most members of the allium family leeks like a rich soil that has had plenty of well rotted manure added prior to planting. Add some lime to gain a pH balance of between 6 and 6.5.

**Maintenance:** As the plants mature the base should be blanched (protected from direct sunlight) to achieve that appetising white appearance. A newspaper collar can be tied around each plant, then the

earth mounded up around them.

**Pests and diseases:** Various mildew and fungal diseases affect members of the allium family, and some precautions may be necessary.

**Harvesting:** Lift plants as needed—they can remain in the ground for quite a time without becoming unpalatable.

## LETTUCE

**Botanical name:** *Lactuca sativa*

**Varieties:** Many varieties including Great Lakes, Pennlake, Yatesdale, Winterlake, Imperial Triumph, Butterhead, Mignonette, Cos (Romaine), Green Cos, Cos Verdi

**Planting:** Can be grown directly in ground from seed, or raised to seedling stage in trays or punnets and transplanted into the garden when large enough to handle. The distance between plants depends on the variety — cos lettuce can be planted quite close together, but larger types need space to mature. There are varieties for planting all year round, although, in hot climates, avoid plantings that are ready for harvesting mid-summer as they will go to seed. Succession planting is advisable to keep a constant supply.

**Requirements:** A humus-rich, moist soil is required for good results. Lettuce grow well in all climates providing the right soil conditions are provided.

**Maintenance:** Protect young plants from snails and slugs, and mulch to keep weed growth down. Water well in summer, and feed every few weeks with a liquid fertiliser to keep growth steady.

**Pests and diseases:** Snails and slugs, and aphids which can spread virus.

**Harvesting:** Pick as soon as the lettuce have a firm heart. If left they will either go to seed or rot, especially if wet. Some varieties can be harvested leaf by leaf to extend the season.

## MELONS

**Botanical name:** *Cucumis melo* var. *reticulata* (rockmelon), *Citrullus vulgaris* (watermelon)

**Varieties:** Hales Best, Rocky Ford, Honeydew, Candy Red

**Planting:** Best sown in small mounds, with three or four seeds together at a depth of 2 cm (³/₄ in). Mounds should be

*Members of the Allium family include (clockwise from top left) white onions, leeks, brown onions, shallots and Spanish onions. They all like rich soil that has been limed prior to planting.*

1 m (3¹/₂ ft) apart. When plants have developed two true leaves, thin to a single, healthy plant. Plant in spring when the soil is warm and the danger of frost has passed.

**Requirements:** A climate with a long, hot summer and not a high rainfall is necessary, unless melons are grown under glass. Rich, moist and well drained soil is also a requirement, so incorporate plenty of organic matter prior to planting.

**Maintenance:** Protect young seedlings from snails and slugs, water well during hot weather and feed every few weeks to keep growth steady, especially when the

flowers first appear. Mulch well to control weeds.

**Pests and diseases:** Squash borer; powdery mildew can be a problem in damp regions.

**Harvesting:** Should be ready for picking towards the end of summer if sown in early spring. When the stem easily separates from the melon, the fruit is well and truly ready.

## ONIONS

**Botanical name:** *Allium cepa*

**Varieties:** Many varieties for planting throughout the year including Early Flat

Barletta, Glaralan, Brown and White Spanish, Cream Gold, Lockyer White and Lockrose

**Planting:** Usually planted in shallow drills 30 cm (1 ft) apart directly in the ground where they are to grow, then later thinned to a distance of 15 cm (6 in) between plants. Some prefer to raise them in a seed tray to seedling stage, transplanting later into the garden bed. There are different varieties for sowing at various times of the year, from late spring to late winter.

**Requirements:** Rich, well drained soil is essential. Add some lime to create a pH balance of between 6 and 6.3.

**Maintenance:** Combating weeds is a problem, especially while seedlings are young. Mulch well, but do not cover the swelling bulbs which need some sunlight. Water well during hot weather.

**Pests and diseases:** Susceptible to onion fly and a variety of fungal diseases. Clean cultivation and crop rotation are effective deterrents.

**Harvesting:** When the foliage turns yellow and wilts, the onions can be harvested. They can be lifted by hand or using a fork. They need to be spread out and dried on a frame until the leaves are brittle. Store in a cool, dry place.

## PARSNIPS

**Botanical name:** *Pastinaca sativa*
**Varieties:** There are several good varieties, including Hollow Crown.
**Planting:** In warm climates spring sowings are advisable, but in temperate to cool climates sow seed directly in the ground in drills during summer for a winter harvest. Drills should be 45 cm (18 in) apart, and the seedlings later thinned out to about 10 cm (4 in) apart.

**Requirements:** Enrich the soil with plenty of well-rotted manure before planting (most other root crops dislike recently manured ground). The soil should be deep and well drained for success.

**Maintenance:** After thinning out seedlings, keep the ground well watered and mulch to keep weed growth down.

**Pests and diseases:** Slugs and snails are a problem at seedling stage. Fungal diseases can occur in humid weather.

**Harvesting:** After 12 weeks parsnips should be ready for harvesting. Pull from the ground and use as needed. Do not allow the remaining crop to stay in the ground too long, or parsnips will become woody.

## PEAS

**Botanical name:** *Pisum sativum* var. *hortense*
**Varieties:** Many varieties including

*Peas (*Pisum sativum *var.* hortense*) are a cool-weather crop that will produce prolifically if good, rich soil conditions are provided. Harvest when pods are young and tender.*

*Potatoes (Solanum tuberosum) are sometimes grown as a first crop to break up the soil in a new garden. They can be mulched with newspaper and straw once the foliage emerges, provided care is taken to cover the tubers as they grow. From left: sweet potato, pontiacs and new potatoes.*

and eaten young, becoming tough and woody if left on the plant. Begin picking from the base of the plant.

## POTATOES
**Botanical name:** *Solanum tuberosum*
**Varieties:** Many varieties including Sebago, Pontiac and Kennebec
**Planting:** Grown from tubers, called seed potatoes, which are old stock with a sprout that has emerged. In cool climates do not plant out until the soil has warmed and the danger of frost has passed. Tubers should be planted in drills 60 cm (2 ft) apart, at a depth of 15 cm (6 in). Allow a distance of 35 cm (14 in) between plants. A large garden is needed to grow potatoes in any quantity.
**Requirements:** Although they can withstand quite poor soils and conditions, potatoes really thrive in a rich moist soil. They are excellent for breaking up uncultivated soil, although some organic matter should be added prior to planting. Do not lime, as potatoes prefer an acid pH level.
**Maintenance:** Keep watering plants in hot weather, and mulch around the base to ensure the tubers are completely protected from the sun. Additional fertiliser will improve the quality of the crop.
**Pests and diseases:** Quite hardy if the right growing conditions are provided.
**Harvesting:** Harvest crops only as they are needed, which can be from 12 weeks after sowing. Leaving some in the ground ensures a continuous supply, and while underground they are still growing!

William Massey, Earlicrop and Greenfeast plus Sugar Peas (*P. sativum* var. *sacharatum*), Snap Peas and Asparagus Peas (*Lotus tetragonolobus*) .
**Planting:** Peas can be sown all year round in cool to cold climates, but are a winter crop in warmer regions. They are generally propagated from seed sown directly where the plants are to grow, 5 cm (2 in) apart, and are given some support on which to climb.
**Requirements:** Rich, moist soil is essential, with a pH balance of approximately 6.5, so add lime if this has not been done the previous season.
**Maintenance:** Mulch to keep weeds down, and water well during warm weather. Encourage the young plants to climb.
**Pests and diseases:** Prone to fungal diseases including stem rot if the conditions are too humid. Protect against thrips and attack by birds.
**Harvesting:** Peas are best when picked

## PUMPKIN

**Botanical name:** *Cucurbita maxima*

**Varieties:** Many varieties from small Butternut to large Queensland Blue.

**Planting:** Seeds can be planted in early spring when frosts have passed. In cool climates raise to seedling stage indoors and transplant when the ground has warmed. Allow at least 60 cm (2 ft) between plants. Rich soil is required, so incorporate plenty of well-rotted manure and compost before planting.

**Maintenance:** Chip away weeds from the base of young plants with care, then mulch to suppress further weed growth. When the trailing shoots are 90 cm (3 ft) long, the growth tips can be pinched out to encourage fruit production. Water well during hot weather, and apply a side-dressing of fertiliser when flowers begin to form.

**Pests and diseases:** Young plants are attacked by snails and slugs (and squash borers in some areas). Leaves may wilt in hot weather.

**Harvesting:** Do not attempt to pick fruits until foliage and stems die back. Most are ready for picking in autumn.

## RADISH

**Botanical name:** *Raphanus sativus*

**Varieties:** Many varieties including Round Red, Cherry Belle, French Breakfast, Long White Icicle and Long Scarlet.

**Planting:** Seeds are sown in shallow drills, no more than 2 cm (³/₄ in) deep, covered with light soil and kept lightly moist until germination. Small seedlings, when large enough to handle, can be thinned to 5 cm (2 in) apart.

**Requirements:** One of the easiest root crops to cultivate, radishes like a well drained soil not freshly manured, with a pH of between 6 and 6.4 (add some lime if this has not been done the previous season).

**Maintenance:** Weeds can be a problem, so mulch the surrounding area. Keep well watered to ensure rapid growth.

**Pests and diseases:** Quite hardy; not prone to infestations.

**Harvesting:** Must be pulled and eaten when young and tender, usually four or five weeks from sowing the seed.

*Pumpkins* (Cucurbita maxima) *are a rewarding crop to grow, although they require space to spread. Varieties include (clockwise from left) Jap, butternut, Jarrahdale and golden nugget.*

# RHUBARB

**Botanical name:** *Rheum rhaponticum*

**Planting:** This excellent perennial is generally grown from roots planted in autumn or winter, when the plant is dormant. Allow 90 cm (3 ft) between each plant, planting firmly and covering with a good mulch of well-rotted manure or compost.

**Requirements:** Must have good, rich soil and moist growing conditions. Add organic matter to the soil prior to planting, and water well during summer. At the end of the growing season when the stalks die back cover the soil surface with a rich organic mulch. In summer a routine application of liquid fertiliser will ensure a good, steady supply of stalks.

**Pests and diseases:** Protect from snails and slugs when young. Watch for crown rot in humid conditions.

**Harvesting:** As required, pull stalks at the base, taking two or three from each plant. Over-harvesting will result in weakened plants the following season.

# SHALLOTS (GREEN BUNCHING ONIONS)

**Botanical name:** *Allium cepa*

**Varieties:** White Lisbon

**Planting:** Sometimes called salad onions, shallots are onions sown close together and harvested young. Best sown in drills with seed scattered at a depth of 2 cm (³⁄₄in).

**Requirements:** Has the same growing requirements as onions.

**Maintenance:** Mulch between drills to keep weed growth down, and water well, especially in hot weather.

*Silver beet* (Beta vulgaris *var.* cicla) *has a high vitamin and mineral content, making it a good year-round crop, even in a small garden. Leaves can be harvested individually.*

**Pests and diseases:** As for onions.
**Harvesting:** Pull shallots when young and tender. Successive plantings should ensure a steady supply.

## SILVER BEET (SWISS CHARD)

**Botanical name:** *Beta vulgaris* var. *cicla*
**Varieties:** Fordhook Giant, Rainbow Chard.
**Planting:** This hardy leaf crop is sometimes mistakenly called spinach. Silver beet can be grown directly in the ground from seed, or as seedlings raised in trays and later transplanted into the garden. Allow a distance of 40 cm (16 in) between the plants. Successive sowings can be made from spring onwards.
**Requirements:** Rich, moist soil with a pH level of between 6.5 and 6.8 is ideal. Add plenty of well-rotted manure prior to planting.
**Maintenance:** Mulch around plants to prevent weed growth, and feed routinely to keep leaf growth steady.
**Pests and diseases:** Protect from snails and slugs when plants are young.
**Harvesting:** Can be harvested leaf by leaf, by cutting at the base with a clean, sharp knife.

## SPINACH

**Botanical name:** *Spinacia oleracea*
**Varieties:** English hybrid, Giant Leaved Winter.
**Planting:** Can be planted in both spring and autumn in most climates. Allow a distance of 15 cm (6 in) between plants. Grow either from seed sown directly in the ground, or from seedlings transplanted when 10 cm (4 in) high.
**Requirements:** Spring plantings should be made in beds with semi-shade to prevent a setback or bolting to seed during hot summer weather. Autumn plantings should be made in full sun. A rich soil with a pH between 6.5 and 6.8 is ideal.
**Maintenance:** Mulch plants when established, feed every three weeks with a liquid fertiliser and water well in summer.
**Pests and diseases:** Protect young plants from snails and slugs and watch for downy mildew.
**Harvesting:** Pick leaves as needed, using a clean, sharp knife to cut from the base of the plant.

## SWEDE (RUTABAGA)

**Botanical name:** *Brassica campestris* var. *rutabaga*
**Varieties:** Early White Vienna, Early Purple.
**Planting:** In cool areas spring to summer sowings are advised; in warmer districts seeds should be sown in late summer. Seeds should be planted 30 cm (12 in) apart. Rich soil with a pH level of between 6.5 and 6.8 is ideal. Add lime and compost prior to planting.
**Maintenance:** Keep the ground around the young plants free from weeds, and mulch and water well during dry periods. An occasional liquid fertiliser will help keep growth steady.
**Pests and diseases:** Boron deficiency can cause brown heart disease.
**Harvesting:** Can be left in the ground and simply dug up as needed. Summer-sown crops will be ready for pulling from mid-winter onwards.

## SWEET CORN

**Botanical name:** *Zea mays* var. *saccharata*
**Varieties:** Iochief hybrid, Golden Cross Bantam, NK195, Super Gold, Honey-sweet.
**Planting:** Although seedlings are commercially available, corn is really best grown directly from seed. The seeds are large and easy to handle and need to be sown in rows 60 cm (2 ft) apart. As a warm-season crop it should be sown in spring when all danger of frost has passed. The soil must be rich and well drained, with some lime added prior to sowing.
**Maintenance:** Keep the soil around the plants weed-free, and mulch to help retain soil moisture. In hot, dry weather soak the ground thoroughly, and mulch with organic matter to support the root systems which become exposed as the stalks grow.
**Pests and diseases:** Caterpillars can be a problem to young plants.
**Harvesting:** Well-grown corn should be ready for harvesting in ten weeks from sowing. Pull back the husks to check that the corn is ripe—as a general rule when the silks turn brown it is time to harvest. Only pick corn as needed, as it is at its best cooked and eaten fresh.

## TOMATOES

**Botanical name:** *Lycopersicon esculentum*
**Varieties:** Many varieties including grafted stock, egg tomatoes, bush tomatoes and cherry tomatoes.

**Planting:** Warm growing conditions are essential for tomatoes, and if the climate is cold these conditions must be created artificially. If planted against a sheltered wall that receives full sun, tomatoes will ripen within the growing season. One trick is to create a warm shelter with bales of hay which will absorb and distribute the heat (the hay can be mulched when the crop has been harvested). Plant in early spring. In cool climates raise seeds to advanced seedling stage and only plant out when the ground has warmed and the danger of frost has passed. Enrich the soil with plenty of organic matter, and add some general fertiliser prior to planting. Stake each plant.

**Maintenance:** Tomatoes require careful maintenance to produce a good crop. As the plants grow they will need to be tied to the stake for support. To encourage a good crop pinch out all lateral growths, and feed with a general fertiliser every few weeks. Water well at ground level, and mulch to keep weed growth down.

**Pests and diseases:** Fertile soil and crop rotation will help prevent disease. Watch for red spider and tomato mosaic virus.

**Harvesting:** Allow tomatoes to ripen fully on the plant. If the autumn weather has started to get cold cut the string holding the plants to their stakes, and lay them out on a bed of straw. Cover with clear plastic or glass cloches, and the remaining fruits will quickly ripen.

## SWEET POTATO
**Botanical name:** *Ipomoea batatas*
**Varieties:** Centennial and Sweet Gold (orange flesh); White Maltese and Coleambarry (white flesh)
**Planting:** Plant tubers in spring, or in cold climates when the danger of heavy frost has passed, in well-prepared soil allowing a distance of 30 cm (1 ft) between plants. In tropical climates a second sowing can be made in summer.
**Maintenance:** The soil must not be allowed to dry out completely during growth, and weeds must be kept under control. Do this either by light cultivation on a weekly basis, or by mulching well around plants. Water deeply twice a week if necessary.
**Pests and diseases:** Watch for aphids which can spread disease, and potato scab which will occur if the soil dries out. Use

*The flavour of fresh home-grown tomatoes (Lycopersicon esculentum) is hard to surpass. Popular varieties include (clockwise from left) egg tomato, vine-ripened tomato, cherry tomato. and yellow pear*

*Harvest zucchini* (Cucurbita pepo) *when small and tender, as they will become tasteless if allowed to remain on the vine. Varieties include Blackjack and the grey Lebanese zucchini.*

certified seed only, to prevent virus diseases.

**Harvesting:** Orange-fleshed sweet potatoes can be ready for harvesting after 16 weeks, while the white-fleshed varieties take up to 40 weeks to mature. Use a fork to lift them, then dry in the sun for a few hours before storing.

## TURNIPS

**Botanical name:** *Brassica campestris* var. *rapa*
**Varieties:** Many varieties including Purple Top, White Globe, White Stone, Foliage or Shagoin.
**Planting:** Turnips should be grown quickly, so a deep, rich and well drained soil is essential. A pH level of between 6.5 and 6.8 is also required. The best results are achieved by growing from seed sown directly in the ground in drills 30 cm (1 ft) apart and thinned (as for carrots) when seedlings are 10 cm (4 in) tall. Allow 8 cm (3 in) between plants, then thin again later so that each plant has a 15 cm (6 in) space around it. Sowings can begin in spring and continue through until autumn.
**Maintenance:** Thin seedlings and then mulch around plants to prevent weed growth. Water well during hot weather.

**Pests and diseases:** Protect from white cabbage butterfly and cabbage moth.
**Harvesting:** When roots have developed to larger than a golf ball size, pull plants and use as needed. Do not allow plants to remain in the ground too long, or they will become tough and woody.

## ZUCCHINI

**Botanical name:** *Cucurbita pepo*
**Varieties:** Many varieties including Blackjack, Greyzini and Golden Zucchini.
**Planting:** These small marrows are easy to grow in a wide range of soils and climates. Incorporate some organic matter into the soil before planting, and allow a distance of 50 cm (20 in) between plants. Can be grown from either seed or seedlings.
**Maintenance:** Mulch around established plants to prevent weed growth, and water well during hot weather. Do not overwater as this can cause fungal diseases and rotting of fruits. A weekly feed of liquid fertiliser will keep plants growing quickly.
**Pests and diseases:** Protect from snails and slugs when plants are young. Watch for downy mildew and powdery mildew. Squash borer is evidenced by severe wilting of the leaves and sawdust-like residue at the base of the stem and/or petioles. Lava must be removed by slitting the stem and extracting it. Bury the damaged stem in good soil and keep watered as new roots will develop.
**Harvesting:** Always harvest fruits when young—between 10-20 cm (4-8 in) in length. If left on the plant they will become marrows. Frequent picking helps to encourage more flowering and fruit.

# THE HERB
# GARDEN

# A Brief History

Herbs have been cultivated and used for medicinal and culinary purposes since Egyptian times. As early as 2700 BC various herbs were grown in the fertile soil by the Nile River, and used to make ointments and potions with a wide range of applications, from embalming the dead to healing the sick. Although the early medicinal use of herbs was based on trial and error, modern scientists are regularly proving the truth behind the success of many of these old healing techniques.

From the Middle East and the Mediterranean, herbs were cultivated in Europe and in Britain, then later in the New World. There is evidence of ancient herbal writings pre-dating the Danish invasions in Britain, and different herbs were later introduced by the conquering Romans.

*OPPOSITE: Thyme* (Thymus) *is available in many varieties, each with different flower colours, foliage and fragrance.*

*PREVIOUS PAGE: Fragrant lavender* (Lavandula spica) *is a worthwhile addition to the herb garden, providing colour, and flowers which can be picked and dried for pot pourri.*

*Both flowers and foliage of nasturtium* (Tropaeolum) *are edible with a strong peppery flavour. Nasturtiums can be easily integrated into the herb or vegetable garden.*

During the Middle Ages monks cultivated and used herbs extensively, making rich liqueurs to cure a wide range of ailments. In the 16th and 17th centuries herbalism was widespread and popular, with names such as Nicholas Culpeper recorded as prominent exponents of herbal craft. Although uneducated and therefore unable to keep records themselves, women were the keepers of knowledge about herbs and their healing powers during this period. The works of Paracelsus were in fact compilations of the knowledge of 'wise women' who knew the virtues and practised the use of herbs.

The early settlers to both America and Australia took herb seeds with them, and they were quickly propagated and spread across the countryside. Needless to say the aboriginal people of both countries had already found their own medicinal uses for various native plants, and some of these remedies were used to heal early European immigrants.

Today herbs are grown extensively for cooking and creating simple recipes to use in herbal baths, hair rinses and fragrant oils. Care must be taken when using herbs medicinally, as some can be toxic even in quite small quantities. Herbs can be harvested and eaten fresh, or dried and stored for later use. They have a more concentrated flavour after drying.

Consider using herbs to make inexpensive gifts. They can be used to flavour oils and vinegars, dried and made into aromatic sachets or pillows, or mixed with other ingredients to make soaps and face creams.

# *Planning, Preparing & Planting*

Like any garden, a herb garden requires some pre-planning and preparation to be successful. Herbs are attractive plants in their own right, often with interesting foliage and flowers, many extremely fragrant. Therefore they can be grown as ornamental species throughout the garden, mingling with annuals, perennials and shrubs.

Alternatively herbs can be grown in a separate bed reserved just for the purpose. This bed should be located in a warm, sunny position, with some shelter from winds. A sheltered rock garden is an excellent way of presenting herbs, with pockets of good soil between the rocks and plants arranged according to their size and growing habit. Larger herbs should be positioned at the back. Those that cascade should be positioned where their foliage can fall over rocks or boulders.

A more traditional walled herb garden is also popular, with herbs arranged in neat beds, and usually labelled for easy identification. Small paths through this formal herb garden can be made of brick or stone, generally following a traditional cottage-garden pattern. A walled garden is of particular benefit in cool to cold climates, as it will act as a suntrap and create a warm micro-climate.

Whichever style of garden you choose, ensure that the ground is well prepared prior to planting out.

## THE SOIL

In general, herbs prefer a light, sandy soil that has good drainage. The soil, however, should contain sufficient organic matter in the form of well rotted manures or compost, to hold moisture and make nutrients available to the plants.

If drainage is a problem, consider creating built-up beds, using timber or stone edgings above ground level. Plenty of humus will need to be incorporated to lighten and aerate the soil.

Prepare the garden by removing all small rocks, debris and weeds. Lightly turn the soils surface over, and add a layer of organic matter to cover the surface. When working the soil ensure that it is neither too wet nor completely dry. It is easy to damage the soil texture by digging when it is waterlogged, likewise when it is too dry. If it lacks moisture, water the area well the day before you plan to clear and cultivate the soil.

## PLANTING

There are annual and perennial herbs which can be grown side-by-side quite successfully. Annual herbs are available as seed or seedlings, and they are also sold as quite advanced plants in pots, ready for establishing in the garden. Perennial herbs are generally sold in pots ready for planting directly where they are to grow. When planting either type make sure that the soil is slightly damp by watering it the day prior to planting. Make sure that the soil in the pot or seedling punnet or tray is also slightly damp.

Planting should be done either early morning, or in the evening when the sun has moved from the garden. Keep freshly planted herbs well watered and mulched, and protect from harsh sun for the first few days if planting during hot weather.

Most herb gardens are started in spring. Successive planting of the annual species can ensure a steady supply. Once established, growth should be rapid if the soil is fertile. Keep weeds down, and little other maintenance should be required.

## PROPAGATION

Once the garden is established, it is possible to create new plants either for starting a new garden bed or for giving as gifts. Many of the perennial herbs can be easily propagated by division. This involves splitting the plant into two or more sections by using a spade to lift it from the ground. The clump is then separated and the parts replanted. If the herb has formed a large healthy clump it is possible to simply dig a sharp spade into one section and lift it out, leaving the rest of the clump growing undisturbed. Other varieties, such as mint, send out root runners which can be easily detached and potted for replanting at a later stage.

*Where space is limited herbs can be grown successfully in containers located in a warm, open situation. If planted in terracotta, which is porous, they should be watered frequently in hot weather to prevent the soil from drying out.*

Annual herbs eventually flower and go to seed, and these seeds can be gathered and stored for sowing the following season. Non-hybridised herbs will propagate easily, and the seeds should be gathered when the plant has turned brown and virtually died. They can be put in an envelope, marked with variety and date, and kept in a dark dry place until the following spring. Some varieties will simply self-seed and regenerate naturally. As the plant dies the seed scatters and the young seedlings emerge unaided.

## CONTAINER GROWING

Many gardeners grow herbs in pots, which is an excellent idea, especially if space is limited. There are specifically designed terracotta herb pots which are shaped like a tall urn, with holes around the sides for various herbs to emerge. This mini herb garden will do well providing the pot is placed in a warm sheltered position and the potting mixture is light, rich and well drained. Regular watering and feeding is essential, espe-

cially if terracotta pots are used, as they are very porous and dry out quickly. Herbs with a cascading habit look particularly effective as pot plants or hanging baskets, positioned near the kitchen where they can be harvested regularly and easily.

It is an excellent idea to grow mint in a container as it is very invasive in the open garden, and will often swamp other species. Just remember to keep the pot well watered—mint thrives on moisture.

# *Healthful Herbs*

## ANNUAL HERBS

### ANISE

**Botanical name:** *Pimpinella anisum*

**Description:** A small growing herb, reaching 45–60 cm (1–2 ft) in height, with aromatic, serrated (dissected) foliage. The flowers are small and white, followed by brown seeds which have a distinctive aniseed flavour.

**Cultivation:** Requires a sunny but sheltered position, and rich, well-drained soil. Sow seeds in spring and again in summer if required.

**Harvesting:** When the seeds have turned brownish remove the heads before they have time to drop the seed. The seed heads may still need a little drying out, and this is done by exposing them to direct sunlight several times. When completely dry, shake out seeds and store in a tightly lidded jar away from bright light.

**Uses:** Anise seed is used in a wide range of foods including cakes, breads, biscuits (cookies) and salads.

### BASIL

**Botanical name:** *Ocimum basilicum*

**Description:** A leafy medium-size plant, growing to 75 cm (2½ ft) with mid-green aromatic foliage. There is also a smaller form, *Ocimum minimum*, or bush basil, which only reaches 30 cm (1 ft) in height, and has a more compact and dense shape.

**Cultivation:** Requires a rich well drained soil and warm growing conditions, plus plenty of water, especially during summer. To keep foliage production going pinch out the flowerheads before the small white blooms have a chance to appear. Sow seeds in spring. In hot climates successive plantings can be made until autumn.

**Harvesting:** Simply remove foliage as needed to use fresh, or dry and store for later use.

**Uses:** Because of its strong, distinctive flavour, basil is popular in many recipes, especially of Mediterranean foods.

### BORAGE

**Botanical name:** *Borago officinalis*

**Description:** A most attractive plant, growing to 90 cm (3 ft) with grey-green foliage and pretty heads of clear-blue flowers. Both leaves and stems are covered with prickly hairs.

**Cultivation:** Likes a warm, sheltered position, and can be grown in semi-shade. The soil must be deep and well drained, with plenty of organic matter added prior to planting. Sow seeds in spring in cold climates; successive sowings are possible in warmer climates.

**Harvesting:** The stems containing foliage and flowers can be picked in late summer and hung to dry, or used fresh. Cooking helps to remove the prickly texture of the foliage.

**Uses:** The leaves, both fresh and dried, are used in a wide range of recipes. The flowers can be crystallised and used for decorative purposes.

### CHERVIL

**Botanical name:** *Anthriscus cerefolium*

**Description:** A pretty herb with light green feathery foliage that has a distinctive aroma and flavour. In the right conditions, it grows to 30 cm (2 ft). Small white flowers appear and eventually go to seed. The plant may happily re-seed and appear the following season.

**Cultivation:** A warm, sheltered position is essential, with some protection from direct summer sun in warmer climates. The soil must be moderately rich with good drainage.

**Harvesting:** The foliage can be picked and eaten fresh as required, like parsley. It can also be dried at the end of the season and stored for later use.

**Uses:** Often used in French recipes, or as part of a 'bouquet of fines herbes'. Used most frequently to flavour omelettes, fish and chicken dishes.

## CORIANDER

**Botanical name:** *Coriandrum sativum*

**Description:** Another leafy herb, growing to 45-60 cm (1.5-2 ft) in height, with tall stems topped by delicate white flowerheads. The leaves, stems and seeds, which are the edible portions of the plant, have a strong aroma and flavour.

**Cultivation:** Like parsley and other leaf herbs, coriander likes a sunny, open position and rich moist soil conditions. Seeds should be sown in spring, although later sowings are permissible in warmer climates.

**Harvesting:** Pick stems and leaves as needed, and pinch out flowerheads if wanting to extend the leaf-producing period. Seeds are collected after the plant has died back. They can be dried and stored in an airtight container

**Uses:** The fresh leaves or crushed seeds are popular in curries and other Asian food. Can be added raw to salads or as an accompaniment to seafoods.

## CUMIN

**Botanical name:** *Cuminum cyminum*

**Description:** A low-growing, slender plant with branching stems and deep green foliage. The flowers, which are

*Coriander (*Coriandrum sativum*), an exotic herb frequently used to flavour Indian and Asian recipes, nevertheless has the same basic growing requirements as the more commonly grown herbs.*

white or rose-coloured, are followed by oblong yellow-brown seeds that are covered with hairs.

**Cultivation:** Rich and well drained soil is essential and a warm climate. Position plant in full sun. Cumin will not withstand dry conditions, so water well in summer.

**Harvesting:** The seeds are harvested and dried, then stored in airtight containers.

**Uses:** Very useful in curries and other Asian foods. The seeds can be used whole, or ground and added to curry pastes.

## DILL

**Botanical name:** *Anethum graveolens*

**Description:** A tall, slender herb growing to 90 cm (3 ft) in height, with pungent blue-green feathery foliage, topped by umbrella-shaped heads of pale yellow flowers. The flowers contain seed which can also be gathered and used for culinary purposes.

**Cultivation:** Choose a sunny, sheltered position and plant in light, well drained soil that has been enriched with some well rotted manure or compost.

**Harvesting:** The foliage can be cut and

*The delicate feathery foliage of dill (*Anethum graveolens*) is excellent in salads. Dill needs full sun, but can survive in a wide range of soil conditions and climates.*

eaten as required, and the seeds gathered by cutting off the flowerheads and drying them in the sun. After drying, the seeds can be gently shaken out and stored in an airtight jar.

**Uses:** The fresh leaves of dill are used extensively, but they can be dried and stored for later use. The seeds are also excellent in a wide range of foods including salads, pastries, breads and sauces.

## FENNEL

**Botanical name:** *Foeniculum vulgare dulce*
**Description:** This herb is often confused with dill, because its appearance is similar. However, fennel foliage is lighter and brighter in colour, and it has a distinctive aniseed flavour—dill has a more peppery taste. Fennel grows to 90 cm (3 ft) in height with feathery foliage topped by umbrella-shaped, bright yellow flowers. The base of the plant is bulbous and white, and this portion of the plant is also edible.

**Cultivation:** Choose a warm sunny position that is sheltered from strong winds. The soil must be rich and moist, and the plant mulched with well rotted manure to force the swollen bulb at the base. Blanch the bulb by covering it with manure and soil mixed together, and water well.

**Harvesting:** The entire plant can be cut from the base when the bulb is a good size. The foliage can be cut and eaten as required, and if the plant is allowed to flower and seed, the seeds can also be collected and dried.

**Uses:** The chopped leaves are added to a wide range of salads and cooked dishes.

The finely sliced bulbous base is also a wonderful salad accompaniment. The seed, when dried, is combined with breads, pastries and pasta.

# PERENNIAL HERBS

Most perennial varieties will die back at the end of summer, virtually disappearing into the soil. They should be protected in cold climates with a layer of organic mulch, and should be watered occasionally if the winter is dry. In spring the plant will re-emerge, and it should be mulched again and fed to encourage growth of foliage and later flowers.

# BIENNIAL AND PERENNIAL HERBS

## BALM

**Botanical name:** *Melissa officinalis*
**Description:** A shrubby perennial bush growing to 75 cm (2½ ft) covered with mid-green lemon-scented foliage and later small white flowers.

**Cultivation:** Extremely easy to grow in a wide range of soils and conditions, balm (or lemon balm) can become a pest as it quickly self-seeds and spreads through the garden. It is advisable to trim the tops of the stems to prevent flowering.

**Harvesting:** Cut the foliage as required and use fresh, or dry and store for later use.

**Uses:** Frequently used as a seasoning or flavouring for chicken and fish dishes and in fruit salads.

## BAY

**Botanical name:** *Laurus nobilis*
**Description:** Bay trees are evergreen and native to the Mediterranean region, growing to 11 m (40 ft) in the right conditions, with aromatic foliage, and berries that can also be harvested. The leaves are shiny and leathery in texture, and the berries a deep-purple colour.

**Cultivation:** Can be grown in a wide range of soils and conditions, although heavy frost can damage the evergreen foliage.

**Harvesting:** Pick leaves as required and dry in a dark, cool place that is free from moisture. Place the leaves in an airtight jar and store away from light.

**Uses:** An important ingredient of bouquet garni, bay leaves are also used as a flavouring in a wide range of Mediterranean recipes. They should be used sparingly as the flavour is very strong.

## BERGAMOT

**Botanical name:** *Monarda didyma*
**Description:** A bushy perennial shrub growing to 1.2 m (4 ft) with red flowers and mint-like leaves that have a hairy texture.

**Cultivation:** Rich moist soil and an open sunny position are essential for successful growth. Plants will die down after flowering, then re-emerge the following spring.

**Harvesting:** Both the leaves and flowers of bergamot are edible, and should be harvested and used fresh as required.

**Uses:** The leaves are commonly used as a flavouring for pork. The flowers and foliage are also used fresh, chopped finely, as an addition to salads.

## CARAWAY

**Botanical name:** *Carum carvi*

**Description:** An ancient biennial herb growing to 60 cm (2 ft) with feathery foliage and tiny white flowers tinged with pink.

**Cultivation:** Can be grown from seed or seedlings in medium-rich well drained soil, in a sunny position but sheltered from prevailing winds. Plant in spring and prune back in autumn for a second harvest the following year.

**Harvesting:** The autumn pruning is in fact the harvesting of the seeds. Cut the top of the plants with the flowers, and dry thoroughly. When dry the seeds can be shaken out and stored in an airtight container.

**Uses:** Caraway seeds have a sharp, spicy flavour and can be used with meats, and in vegetable dishes, breads and dumplings.

## CAMOMILE

**Botanical name:** *Anthemis nobilis* (Lawn Camomile) *Matricaria chamomilla* (Wild Camomile)

**Description:** Both camomiles have pretty white daisy flowers with yellow centres. Lawn camomile is low-growing and used as a ground-cover or lawn, while wild camomile has a bushy habit, growing to 60 cm (2 ft) with light green foliage and a profusion of flowers. It is often integrated into the flower garden.

*The seeds of the caraway* (Carum carvi) *are harvested in autumn by cutting the flower stems and hanging them to dry. The spicy seeds can then be shaken from the plant and stored for later use.*

**Cultivation:** Treat *Anthemis nobilis* as an annual and *Matricaria chamomilla* as a perennial. Both like moderately rich and well drained soil, and plenty of moisture during summer. Plant in an open, sunny position.

**Harvesting:** The flowers of wild camomile can be picked, and dried in a cool, dry position. Store in an airtight container when thoroughly dry.

**Uses:** The dried flowers are used to make a soothing, refreshing tea.

## CHIVES

**Botanical name:** *Allium schoenoprasum*

**Description:** A popular and widely-cul-

*Chives (*Allium schoenoprasum*) are harvested by cutting at the base with sharp scissors as needed. Allow a good clump to flower and go to seed to ensure a new clump the following season.*

tivated herb growing in a clump to 30 cm (1 ft) with slender green grass-like foliage and topped by circular mauve flowerheads.

**Cultivation:** Plant in a sunny open location in rich soil that has had plenty of organic matter added to it. Water well during hot weather.

**Harvesting:** Use a clean, sharp knife to harvest small bunches of chives as needed, cutting them at ground level.

**Uses:** Used widely as a subtle onion-flavouring in salads and cooked dishes. Garlic chives (*Allium tuberosum*) have a strong garlic aroma, and are popular in Asian recipes. Both should be added to food at the last minute, so their flavour will not be lost.

## COMFREY

**Botanical name:** *Symphytum officinalis*

**Description:** A vigorous clump-forming plant, growing to 1.2 m (4 ft) with large grey-green hairy leaves and slender stems topped by small mauve-pink flowers.

**Cultivation:** Prefers a sunny, open position and moderately fertile, moist soil. Comfrey is very deep-rooted and can be used to break up heavy clay soils, although it is also inclined to be invasive and once it takes hold is hard to remove except by digging deeply and removing all the root material.

**Harvesting:** The foliage can be removed as needed by cutting at the base with a sharp knife. The plant will die back naturally in winter, and re-emerge in spring. Cut stems before flowering to avoid rapid spread by self-seeding.

**Uses:** Some herbalists recommend eating

comfrey, although there are strong arguments against it. Its value in the herb garden is as a green manure crop, or an addition to the compost heap, where it accelerates decomposition.

## GARLIC

**Botanical name:** *Allium sativum*

**Description:** A perennial member of the onion family, with long, flat leaves and tall flower stalks topped by large circular flowerheads that are white, tinged with pink. Beneath the ground is a bulb consisting of cloves, covered with a white membrane.

**Cultivation:** Plant in a sunny position in rich soil with good drainage, and water well during the summer months if the climate is hot and dry. Spring is the usual planting time.

**Harvesting:** When the foliage has shrivelled and died back at the end of summer, the bulbs can be dug up and dried in a cool, shady place.

**Uses:** Surely one of the most popular and widely used flavouring herbs, garlic is especially useful in Italian, French and Asian recipes.

## HORSERADISH

**Botanical name:** *Armoracia rusticana*

**Description:** An attractive leafy plant growing to 30 cm (1 ft) with large light-green leaves emerging from the base. The small white flowers grow in tiny clusters on long stalks, and the fleshy roots are the most commonly used edible portion of the plant.

**Cultivation:** Prefers a sunny, open

*Like all members of the Allium family, garlic* (Allium sativum) *produces a circular flowerhead on top of a slender stalk. Garlic is often planted as an insect repellent, as well as for use as a culinary herb.*

position and moderately rich soil, Water well during hot, dry weather. Protect foliage from snails and slugs, which can be a problem when the plant is young.

**Harvesting:** The roots can be dug up in autumn, and the larger ones stored in a damp, dark place to be used for culinary purposes. If exposed to the light they will turn green. The smaller roots can be stored in a dry place and replanted the following spring.

**Uses:** The young leaves can be finely chopped and added to salads. The roots can be grated and made into a concentrated paste. Store in containers in the refrigerator.

## LEMON GRASS

**Botanical name:** *Cymbopogon citratus*

**Description:** A medium-size clump-forming plant, with masses of slender pale-green grasslike leaves that are slightly sticky to the touch. The foliage has a strong lemon aroma and flavour.

**Cultivation:** As an Asian native, lemon grass prefers a warm to hot climate. Grows well in moderately rich soil and plenty of moisture in summer. Foliage dies back in winter.

**Harvesting:** The tips, shoots and leaves are cut at ground level with a sharp knife as needed.

**Uses:** Used to make a refreshing tea, or chopped and added to a wide variety of curries and other spicy Asian recipes.

## LOVAGE

**Botanical name:** *Levisticum officinale*

**Description:** An ancient perennial herb

that grows to 1.5 m (5 ft) with dark-green shiny leaves borne on straight, hollow stems. The stems are topped by attractive yellow flowerheads.

**Cultivation:** Must have deep, rich and moist soil to grow successfully. Can be cultivated in a wide range of climates and is often used as a windbreak on the border of a herb garden

**Harvesting:** The leaves can be harvested and used fresh as needed. The seeds are also sometimes gathered and stored in an airtight container.

**Uses:** The finely-chopped foliage is used to flavour soups and stews, and is sometimes eaten raw in salads. The seeds have a particularly strong flavour, and should be used in moderation.

## MARJORAM

**Botanical name:** *Origanum marjorana*

**Description:** A useful perennial herb, growing to 45 cm (1½ft) in height, with attractive soft grey-green foliage and tiny white fluffy flowers in summer and autumn. Has an attractive shape and can be used in the ornamental garden to great effect.

**Cultivation:** Prefers a warm, sheltered position and well drained light soil, with sufficient water in summer to prevent the roots drying out completely.

**Harvesting:** The foliage can be cut and eaten fresh as needed, or dried at the end of the season and stored for later use.

**Uses:** A basic herb with many uses, it is an ingredient of 'mixed herbs' together with sage and thyme. The dried form has a stronger flavour than the fresh foliage.

*Marjoram* (Origanum marjorana) *must be grown in a warm, well drained situation, and looks effective as part of a perennial border or rockery garden.*

## MINT

**Botanical name:** *Mentha spicata* (Spearmint); *Mentha piperita officinalis* (Peppermint); *Mentha pulegium* (Pennyroyal); *Mentha piperita citrata* (Eau-de-Cologne mint); *Mentha rotundafolia* (Applemint).

**Description:** There are many forms of mint with different distinctive foliage and flavours. The foliage varies in colour and shape according to variety, and the

*Mint* (Mentha) *can be invasive if allowed to grow in a mixed bed of herbs. Try wedging boards into the ground to contain the roots, or alternatively cultivate the plant in a large container.*

flowers are white, lilac or purple, again according to variety.

**Cultivation:** Rich soil and moist conditions are the major requirement. Choose an open sunny position, and take care to restrict the growing area as most mints are invasive and will swamp other plants. Traditionally mint is grown near a tap or pond to provide access to water. A board pushed into the ground will prevent the root runners from spreading.

**Harvesting:** The foliage can be picked and used fresh as required, or can be dried and stored in an airtight container for later use.

**Uses:** Mint is a popular flavouring herb for a wide range of dishes. The individual varieties have their own particular uses, in sauces, jellies and salads.

## OREGANO

**Botanical name:** *Origanum vulgare*

**Description:** A strongly fragrant herb growing to 60 cm (2 ft) with bright-green coarse-textured foliage and tiny white flowers during summer.

**Cultivation:** Likes sun, although it can also tolerate partial shade. The soil should be light and well drained.

**Harvesting:** Pick and eat the foliage and flowers fresh as required—the flowers have an even more intense flavour than the foliage. At the end of the summer the whole plant can be harvested by cutting the stems back to almost ground level, and hanging them to dry. Store in an airtight container.

**Uses:** Oregano is one of the most popular culinary herbs, favoured in Greek and Italian cooking.

*A Mediterranean herb of distinction, oregano* (Origanum vulgare) *is strongly fragrant and easy to grow in most soils and climates, as long as warmth and shelter are provided. Oregano makes an excellent container specimen.*

## PARSLEY

**Botanical name:** *Petroselinum crispum*
There are several varieties, including Italian parsley (*P. crispum neapolitanum*) and Hamburg parsley (*P. sativum*).
**Description:** This biennial is probably the most popular and widely-used herb grown. It's a small to medium-size leafy plant, grown from seed, with deep-green foliage that differs according to variety.
**Cultivation:** Parsley likes a sunny, open

position and well drained but rich, moist soil. Add plenty of organic matter prior to planting, water well in summer and pick regularly to prevent flowering.
**Harvesting:** Simply pick the leaves as needed, which will also encourage further foliage growth. Pick at the base of the stem—the plant should last through winter and keep producing into a second summer.
**Uses:** Generally added at the last minute to both hot dishes and salads. High in nutritional value, containing Vitamin C and iron.

## ROSEMARY

**Botanical name:** *Rosmarinus officinalis*
**Description:** A perennial shrub, growing to 1.5 m (5 ft) in the right conditions, with narrow grey-green foliage that is highly aromatic, and a profusion of blue flowers in summer.
**Cultivation:** Prefers a moderately rich loam with some lime added, and a sunny, open position. Good drainage is very important.
**Harvesting:** The foliage can be cut as needed and used fresh, or picked in bunches and dried for storage and later use.
**Uses:** The oil contained in the foliage is extracted for commercial use. The foliage is used as a flavouring herb, and is especially popular in lamb dishes.

## SAGE

**Botanical name:** *Salvia officinalis*
**Description:** Another of the popular herbs, an essential for the balanced herb

*Rosemary (*Rosmarinus officinalis*) benefits from frequent picking, which encourages a dense, lush growth of foliage. Bunches can be hung to dry inside, then stored in an airtight container for year-round use.*

garden. There are more than 700 species of sage, which is a hardy medium-size perennial, growing to 90 cm (3 ft) in height. It's a clump-forming plant, and the foliage is grey-green in colour, covered with veins.
**Cultivation:** Prefers a rich slightly heavy textured soil, but good drainage is essential. Position in a sunny, open location.
**Harvesting:** Simply pick and use the foliage fresh as required, or harvest in large bunches and dry for later use.

Uses: Popular as a seasoning in salads, meat and chicken dishes.

## SAVORY

**Botanical name:** *Satureia montana*
**Description:** A bushy perennial, growing to 30 cm (1 ft) with small white

*With its soft grey-green foliage, sage (Salvia officinalis) forms a visual contrast to herbs with deeper green foliage. The leaves can be harvested and eaten fresh, or dried and stored.*

flowers all through summer. The glossy green aromatic foliage has a slight peppery taste.
**Cultivation:** Plant in a sunny, open position in light, well drained soil. Sometimes grown as a small hedging plant, it is ideal for a herb garden border.
**Harvesting:** The sharp-tasting foliage can be picked and used fresh, or dried and stored for later use.
**Uses:** A useful flavouring for hot or cold vegetable dishes, or as a seasoning for stuffings or pies.

## TARRAGON

**Botanical name:** *Artemisia dracunculus*
**Description:** A bushy, tangled perennial, growing to 90 cm (3 ft) with spicy-fragrant foliage and flowers that don't mature or bear seed. The foliage and stems die back in winter.
**Cultivation:** Locate tarragon in a sunny position in rich, light soil. When the foliage dies back in early winter mulch the roots well and mark the spot to prevent accidental digging-up of the roots. Water well.
**Harvesting:** Like most herbs the leaves can be picked and used fresh, or can be harvested and dried for storage and later use.
**Uses:** A popular herb in French cooking, used to flavour vinegars, dressings, sauces and a wide range of meat and vegetable dishes.

## THYME

**Botanical name:** *Thymus vulgaris*
**Description:** An attractive low-growing perennial, reaching 30 cm (1 ft) in height,

with spreading stems covered with light grey-green strongly aromatic foliage and tiny creamy-pink spring flowers. Other varieties are Lemon Thyme (*T. citriodorus*) and Wild Thyme (*T. serpyllum*).
**Cultivation:** Plenty of sun and light, and a sandy soil are essential for success. The more gritty the soil, the better the results. Avoid shady and damp conditions. Thyme is often grown as a ground cover in garden beds, or as a lawn alternative in warm, sunny positions.
**Harvesting:** Pick and use foliage fresh, or dry bunches and store in an airtight container for later use.
**Uses:** One of the major herbs, a basic ingredient of bouquet garni and mixed herbs. Usually added fresh at the beginning of the cooking process, so that the flavour can be absorbed.

## WATERCRESS

**Botanical name:** *Nasturtium officinale*
**Description:** A delicious perennial with a biting, peppery flavour, watercress grows to 45 cm (1¹/₂ft) sending out long stems that are covered in dark-green glossy leaves and tiny white flowers.
**Cultivation:** Must have damp conditions to grow successfully, although a stagnant pond is not suitable. Instead plant in rich, damp soil where water can run across the roots. To keep the foliage production going pinch back flowerheads as they appear
**Harvesting:** Pick the stems and use fresh. It is not suitable for drying.
**Uses:** A valuable source of vitamins, biting and fresh in flavour, used as an ingredient of salads or soups.

# The
# BACKYARD
# ORCHARD

# Growing Fruit

Growing fruit adds an extra dimension to the productive garden. Even a small inner-city courtyard garden has space for a citrus tree or two, and if well grown they will produce a good yield over many months.

Consider growing fruiting plants instead of ornamental varieties as part of the garden landscape. Although tradition says that fruiting trees must be heavily pruned, this can be done to preserve the natural shape and line of the tree. Stonefruit trees have glorious spring blossoms, and if well cared for will look attractive all year round. Apart from fruiting trees, there are many shrubs, vines and brambles that bear fruit and require a minimum of attention.

The main disadvantage of fruit growing is the necessity for spraying pesticides and fungicides at various stages of growth. This can be avoided to a great extent if organic preventative measures are taken, and clean cultivation methods are observed.

*OPPOSITE: Japanese plums* (Prunus salicina) *are trouble free and can be grown in all but the warmest climates. They are favoured by organic gardeners because they are generally disease and pest resistant.*

*PREVIOUS PAGE: Raspberries* (Rubus idaeus) *like mild summers and cool to cold winters. Well-grown plants will produce berries over many weeks in summer.*

*Apples* (Malus pumila), *crisp, and delicious, will become infested with fruit fly if fallen fruit is allowed to rot on the ground. Rake regularly under the trees in autumn.*

# *Planning & Planting*

Fruiting crops all require full sun and good growing conditions to produce results. When deciding on the placement of trees, vines, shrubs or brambles, this factor should be taken into consideration. Remember also that these plants will require plenty of space as they mature. Do not place large-growing fruiting trees too close together, unless you intend to prune them considerably, or they will overlap and prevent sunlight from reaching the fruit. Without sunlight the fruit will take much longer to ripen.

Plant only fruits that do well in your particular climate. Choose a warm and sheltered position, with some protection against strong winds or winter frosts. It is possible, of course, to grow a particular fruiting variety in a climate that isn't ideal, providing the plants are given extra protection. However, these plants will always be more susceptible to pests and disease infestation, and will require constant monitoring if they are to produce. In the long term it's best to plant tropical fruits in a tropical climate, and cool-climate fruits in a cool climate !

In a cold climate, young fruiting trees may need protection. A simple hessian (burlap) frost cover will be enough to shelter the tree from both spring frosts, which can damage soft, new growth, and autumn frosts, which will damage late maturing fruits. When the tree has become well established, after two years or more, this protection should no longer be necessary.

## PLANTING

Deciduous fruiting trees are generally bought bare-rooted for planting in the dormant months, from late autumn to early spring. However, some nurseries stock potted fruit trees all year round. Select healthy, well shaped trees and plant them immediately they are brought home from the nursery. Although the roots of bare-rooted trees are packed in a moisture-retaining medium, there is always a risk that this could dry out and the tree be killed.

Choose a position with good drainage and dig a hole that is deep and wide enough to accommodate the full spread of the roots. The soil at the base of the hole should be broken up to allow root penetration when growing begins. Well rotted manure or compost mixed with the soil from the hole will provide a rich basis for early growth

If the tree requires staking (and this is a good idea for most varieties) place the stake in the hole at planting time. Hammering a stake in after the event can damage the root system. Position the tree with care so that the main trunk is in line with the stake, and fill in and around with the soil/compost mixture. After planting, water well, and mulch with organic matter to suppress weed growth and to help keep the soil moist.

Fruiting vines, berries and bushes also require careful planting to remain healthy. Ensure that the area where they are to be planted is free from weed growth, and dig a large enough hole to comfortably accommodate the spreading roots. The addition of well rotted organic matter into the ground at planting time will help ensure success.

Most fruiting varieties resent grass growth at their base. A continuous mulching program will help keep lawn from invading their root systems and competing for moisture and nutrients.

## WATERING AND FEEDING

In hot and dry climates, irrigation will be necessary. Plants are best watered deeply once a week to encourage their roots to travel downwards in search of moisture. Shallow watering has the reverse effect, and will encourage shallow-rooted plants.

Mulch will help keep the moisture under the ground, especially if hot, drying winds are a problem.

Most fruiting plants appreciate the addition of a fertiliser once or twice a year. Early spring is a good time to feed plants, to boost spring growth, and again if needed when the fruit has set. Base the feeding regime on the needs of the individual plant. Plants in harsh climates or depleted soils will obviously require more feeding that those grown in deep, rich loam in a moist climate.

## PRUNING

Deciduous fruiting trees are generally pruned in winter. Pruning helps to keep the tree a manageable size for harvesting, and also encourages larger fruits. Most home fruit producers prefer pruning to an open vase-shape, which allows easy access to fruit at harvest time, and allows sun and air to penetrate and hasten ripening. Use clean, sharp secateurs (pruners) and follow the instructions for each variety.

*LEFT: Fruiting trees can be ornamental as well as productive. Position them so they can be admired and enjoyed.*

# Fruits Of The Field

## APPLES

**Botanical name:** *Malus pumila*

**Requirements:** Popular because they can be grown in a wide range of soils and climates, although they prefer a cold winter. Many varieties that will fruit at different times, and are suited to different growing conditions. Good drainage is important, as is protection from strong winds. Most apples are self-sterile, so two varieties will be needed to cross-pollinate.

**Pruning:** In winter, prune trees to a vase-shape. A young tree will take several years to shape. Fruit is borne on two-year-old wood, and the aim of pruning is to encourage the growth of these fruit-bearing stems.

**Pests and diseases:** Some gardeners advocate an intensive spraying program against fungal diseases, black spot and fruit fly. However, clean cultivation and good growing conditions can prevent many such problems. See organic alternatives on page 121.

*RIGHT: Late cropping Granny Smiths are delicious fresh or made into sauces, pies or preserves.*

## APRICOTS

**Botanical name:** *Prunus armeniaca*

**Requirements:** Likes a climate with warm summers and cool winters. A dry spring and summer are useful, as fruit tends to split if there is too much moisture. The soil should be an average loam, well drained, with organic matter added at planting time.

**Pruning:** Prune to a vase-shape in winter.

**Pests and disease:** Brown rot, rust and fruit fly can be a problem in certain areas.

## BLUEBERRIES

**Botanical name:** *Vaccinium*

**Requirements:** A cool to cold climate is important for successful budburst in spring. Prefers a strongly acid, peaty soil that is well drained but remains moist, especially during summer. Feed late winter to early spring.

**Pruning:** Do not prune during the first three years. Fruit is borne on the previous year's wood. Cut from one to four of the oldest shoots on each bush to encourage new shoot growth.

**Pests and diseases:** Birds can be a problem as fruit ripens. Try covering bushes with a net.

## CHERRIES

**Botanical name:** *Prunus avium*

**Requirements:** Like most deciduous fruiting trees and bushes, cherries do best in a climate that has cool to cold winters, although they can still be grown successfully in more temperate regions. Good soil conditions are important. Ensure that the ground is deep, well drained and rich with organic matter. Two compatible trees are needed for pollination.

**Pruning:** Light pruning only, to open out the shape. Do not prune in winter. Brown rot can be a problem.

## CURRANTS

**Botanical name:** *Ribes nigrum* (black) *sativum* (red and white)

**Requirements:** A deciduous shrub which prefers a cold winter climate, but can nevertheless be damaged by late

*Cherries are usually the first fruits of summer. Two compatible trees will be needed for pollination. In smaller gardens neighbours sometimes co-operate to each cultivate a fruit-bearing tree.*

*Red currants* (Ribes sativum) *are cool-climate fruits borne on small deciduous bushes which make an excellent low hedge or windbreak for the vegetable garden. The bushes can be pruned in winter.*

spring frosts. Enrich the soil with plenty of organic matter prior to planting.

**Pruning:** With black currants the fruit is borne on the last season's young wood. The aim in pruning is to cut out old, dark wood to encourage new shoots to grow. This should be done in winter when the bushes are dormant. White and red currants are produced on old wood,

and little pruning is required.

**Pests and diseases:** Not generally susceptible.

## GRAPEFRUIT

**Botanical name:** *Citrus x paradisi*

**Requirements:** Sensitive to cold climates, grapefruit resents frost and care will need to be taken to protect them.

Like all citrus they need a fertile soil with good drainage.

**Pruning:** Remove sucker growth at the grafting point, then cut out any dead or diseased wood to keep the tree shape open.

**Pests and diseases:** Aphids can introduce the virus tristeza in certain climates. Ask for disease-resistant strains.

*Deciduous grapes* (Vitis vinifera) *are frequently grown as an ornamental climber, with the fruits simply an added bonus. Varieties include (left to right) black muscat, Waltham Cross and Cornichon.*

## GRAPES

**Botanical name:** *Vitis vinifera*

**Requirements:** These deciduous vines are suitable for growing in most climates that Do not experience a high summer rainfall. Too much summer rain encourages fungal diseases. Ideally the climate should be warm to hot, and not too wet. Vines can either be grown informally over a pergola or trellis, or trained professionally on a timber and wire support. The soil must be rich and well drained, with plenty of organic matter added.

**Pruning:** Fruit is borne on new season's shoots, arising from two-year-old wood. Severity of pruning will depend on how the grapes are grown. All pruning is done in winter.

**Pests and diseases:** Various mildew diseases can be a problem. Spray with sulphur as an alternative to fungicides.

*Citrus fruits such as (clockwise from top) grapefruit, mandarin, orange, lime and lemon grow best in climates that have warm to hot summers and mild winters. Water well in summer.*

## LEMONS

**Botanical name:** *Citrus limon*

**Requirements:** Very useful small trees, requiring little space and producing fruits over many months of the year. There are varieties for most climate conditions, including even very cold climates. Good soil conditions are essential, and frequent feeding with a specially formulated citrus food will bring good results.

**Pruning:** Remove suckers that emerge at the base of the trunk, then prune out dead wood from the centre as required.

**Pests and diseases:** If grown in good conditions lemons are quite hardy. Most problems arise from nutrient deficiencies.

## LIMES

**Botanical name:** *Citrus aurantifolia*

**Requirements:** Very frost-sensitive, limes need warm sheltered conditions. Rich soil with good drainage is essential.

**Pruning:** Remove dead wood from the centre of the tree if necessary.

**Pests and diseases:** Ensure the right growing conditions to prevent problems.

*Stone fruits such as (from left) peach, plum and nectarine are best cultivated in a cool climate. The trees are deciduous, producing glorious blossoms in early spring.*

## MANDARINS

**Botanical name:** *Citrus reticulata*

Requirements: Slightly more frost-sensitive than oranges, mandarins can nevertheless be grown in cool climates if shelter and warmth are provided. Ensure soil is rich, with plenty of organic matter added before planting, and then added afterwards as a routine mulch.

**Pruning:** Only to remove dead wood.

**Pests and diseases:** Watch for fungal diseases in warm, moist climates.

## NECTARINES

**Botanical name:** *Prunus persica* var. *nectarina*

**Requirements:** Slightly less hardy than its close relative the peach. Otherwise requirements identical.

**Pruning:** As for peaches.

**Pests and diseases:** As for peaches.

## ORANGES

**Botanical name:** *Citrus sinensis*

**Requirements:** Although they prefer a warm to hot climate, oranges are quite adaptable and can withstand light frost if some protection is provided. They prefer a cool winter and warm to hot summer. Soil must be rich and well drained.

**Pruning:** Let light into the tree by pruning out dead wood from the centre.

**Pests and diseases:** Like all citrus, oranges are prone to fungal disease in poor growing conditions. Nutrient deficiencies can create a range of problems.

*Pears* (Pyrus communis) *like cool to cold winters and a warm summer. Plant in a sunny position where the soil is well drained. From top: Beurre bosc, Packham, Tosca.*

## PEACHES

**Botanical name:** *Prunus persica*

**Requirements:** The ideal climate for peaches is a warm to hot summer followed by a cool to cold winter. They can be grown in a wide range of soils, providing drainage is adequate.

**Pruning:** Prune to a vase-shape in winter. Fruit is produced on one-year-old shoots, and young trees should start producing a good quantity of fruits the third year from planting.

**Pests and diseases:** Leaf curl, rust, brown rot and fruit fly are just some of the problems affecting peaches and nectarines. Can be grown organically with great care, or a routine spraying program.

## PEARS

**Botanical name:** *Pyrus communis*

**Requirements:** Pears have the same basic climate requirements as apples—a winter that is cool to cold, a spring with light rainfall and a warm summer. Rich, well drained loam is essential. Pear trees take several years to reach maturity, not producing a heavy crop until about seven years from planting.

**Pruning:** A light annual pruning gives the best results. Prune in winter, creating an open vase-shape.

**Pests and diseases:** Pear scab and codling moths are problems to watch for. Avoid wet conditions and use clean cultivation methods to prevent problems.

## PLUMS

**Botanical names:** *Prunus domestica* (European), *P. salicina* (Japanese), *P. cerasifera* (cherry plum).

**Requirements:** The European plum requires cooler growing conditions than the Japanese varieties. Both types need a winter cool enough to induce dormancy. Can be grown in a wide range of soils and conditions, even tolerating quite damp ground that would normally badly affect stone fruit trees.

**Pruning:** Pruning is not essential to fruit-bearing, although commonly trees are pruned back to a vase-shape in winter.

**Pests and diseases:** Plums are more hardy than most stone fruits, however keep the ground clear of fallen fruits to prevent fruit fly.

## RASPBERRIES

**Botanical name:** *Rubus idaeus*

**Requirements:** A cool climate crop, growing best where the summer is mild and the winter cool to cold. Moderately rich, well drained soil brings good results. Plants sucker freely and can be invasive if planted near the vegetable garden. Generally grown between two parallel wires and pruned hard during winter.

**Pruning:** After fruiting the old canes are cut back at ground level and the new canes tied to the wire supports. There is generally quite a lot of work involved in maintaining a neat group of plants.

**Pests and diseases:** Although a range of diseases can affect raspberries, if well grown they are generally quite hardy and resilient.

## STRAWBERRIES

**Botanical name:** *Fragaria chiloensis x Fragaria virginiana*

*Healthy strawberry plants (*Fragaria*) will keep producing offsets which can be separated to provide new plants each season. Mulch to keep the developing fruit from touching the soil surface.*

**Requirements:** Can be grown in a wide range of soils, but will not tolerate poor drainage. Most climates are suitable, and new plants can be continually produced by removing and replanting the runners developed after flowering. A very rewarding crop for the home garden.

**Pruning:** Not necessary.

**Pests and diseases:** To ensure the best crop, always buy virus-free plants and protect the fruit from slugs, snails and birds. Mulch plants with straw to support ripening fruit and to prevent mould.

# STORING
# THE
# HARVEST

# *Preserving freshness*

No matter how successful the garden, the benefits cannot be reaped unless harvesting and storing is well organised. The experienced gardener will have employed succession planting to ensure a steady supply —but not over-supply—of various crops such as lettuce. However, there are many crops that are ready for harvesting simultaneously, and this situation means the gardener must learn the various methods of storing the harvest.

## FREEZING

Most vegetables, except those with a high water content, are suitable for freezing. The basic method is to prepare the vegetables by peeling or slicing them as required, then to blanch them in boiling water for approximately one to five minutes. They are then quickly drained and plunged into cold water, drained again, then sealed in plastic bags and immediately frozen.

This method, called 'snap freezing', preserves the vegetables in near-perfect

*OPPOSITE: Store bottled and preserved fruits and vegetables inside a dark cupboard to prevent the contents from fading or spoiling.*

*PREVIOUS PAGE: The most satisfying time for the gardener is when the crops are ready for harvesting.*

*Use only the best quality produce for bottling or making conserves. If fruit is bruised, remove the spoiled portion and use the remainder immediately. Peaches (Prunus persica) are ideal for bottling.*

condition. Only freeze good quality, fresh young vegetables and ensure it is done immediately after harvesting. Do not attempt to freeze produce that has been sitting in the refrigerator for days!

**Suitable crops:** Artichokes, asparagus, eggplants, beans, beetroot (beets), broccoli, brussels sprouts, carrots, cauliflower, onions, parsnips, peas, peppers, spinach, sweetcorn and various fruits.

## DRYING

This is a popular way of preserving fruits and tomatoes. For successful drying always use good quality, fresh and unblemished produce—bruised fruits will rot before they dry! Small-scale drying can be done in the sun, with fruits arranged on slatted timber trays. Never allow individual items to touch each other, and allow plenty of time. Drying is a process that can't be hurried. The secret of success is hot, dry conditions with good air circulation. It is important that all the moisture is removed prior to storing the dried produce. Afterwards it can be stored in airtight containers or, in the case of tomatoes, in seasoned olive oil.

**Suitable crops:** Apples, apricots, grapes, pears, figs, plums, peaches, mushrooms, peppers, garlic, tomatoes.

## PICKLING

Many vegetables are suitable for pickling, which preserves them in vinegar. Select good quality produce and wash and cut it to size before blanching in boiling water. Pack clean glass jars with the blanched vegetables and then cover with vinegar, either plain or seasoned.

**Suitable crops:** Onions, cauliflowers, carrots, cabbage, beetroot (beets), broccoli, peppers, zucchini, celery.

## BOTTLING

This is an old-fashioned but effective method of storing fruits and certain vegetables. Stone fruits are especially good preserved in this way. As with all preserving methods, success depends on using good quality produce. Peel and slice the vegetables, then pack them carefully into sterilised jars. Cover with a prepared sugar and water syrup and seal the preserving jars.

The final stage is the cooking of the produce inside the sealed jar, which should be done under controlled conditions. The jars are immersed in a large pot of water and brought to the boil. They are kept at the boil for a specified time, which varies according to the fruit.

**Suitable crops:** Apples, apricots, blackberries, currants, cherries, plums, figs, gooseberries, loganberries, mulberries, peaches, pears, pineapple, quinces, raspberries, rhubarb, strawberries, tomatoes, beans, peas, carrots.

## CONSERVES OR RELISHES

A creative cook can use garden produce to make a wide variety of jams, marmalades, relishes, chutneys, conserves, fruit cheeses, syrups and jellies. There are endless recipes for these, and it is certainly a good way of using leftover fruits and vegetables. Although it is preferable to use good quality produce, making relishes can be a good way of using less-than-perfect fruits or vegetables and thus avoiding wastage. Always cut out any bruised areas, using only the unblemished part of the produce.

**Suitable crops:** All fruits and vegetables can be incorporated.

## SALTING

Not often used in these days of refrigeration and concern about salt in the diet.

## CANDIED FRUITS

Although not the healthiest method of preserving produce, crystallised, glacé or candied fruit is good for special occasions or celebrations. The process involves soaking and boiling prepared fresh fruits in thick sugar syrup for several days. The fruit eventually absorbs a large amount of sugar and is thus preserved.

**Suitable crops:** Citrus fruit, grapes, cherries, all stone fruits.

## DRYING HERBS

Both annual and perennial herbs can be dried by harvesting the stems and hanging them for several weeks. Use a warm, dry cupboard for this if you can, because it prevents dust from settling in the herbs. Fast drying can be done by laying out the stems of foliage on a wire rack in a low oven for one hour, although essential flavour can be lost. Ideally the herbs should be picked just before they flower, unless they are a variety that has very aromatic flowers. When dry, the foliage should be stripped from the stems and stored in an airtight container.

## STORAGE TIPS

• Potatoes should always be stored away from light in a cool, dry place.
• Pumpkins can be stored in a cool, dry place for several months.

*RIGHT: Herbs should be dried in bunches in a cool, well ventilated location away from direct sunlight. A cloth cover will prevent them from becoming dusty during the drying process.*

# PEST & DISEASE PREVENTION

# *Organic alternatives*

In these days of chemical sprays and formulas it is easy to find a quick-fix solution to any garden ailment. However, these days the thoughtful gardener always looks for an organic alternative rather than drowning plants in chemical mixes.

Manufacturers have responded to this desire for natural gardening, and new products including non-harmful insecticides and fungicides are constantly appearing on the shop shelves.

It is as well to remember that every garden is a small ecosystem, with a fine balance between healthy growth of plants and disease or pest infestation. Insects themselves have a way of working to balance this ecosystem; one type preys on another and this keeps the numbers under control. When we spray against one insect, we invariably also kill others

*OPPOSITE: Commercially grown vegetables are more prone to insect attack and disease than those grown by the home gardener, and therefore require more attention with chemical sprays.*

*PREVIOUS PAGE: Examine plants frequently to detect insects before they become a problem. Here a harlequin bug investigates raspberry (Rubus) foliage.*

*Basil (*Ocimum basilicum*) and marigolds (*Tagetes*) are good organic insect repellants. Plant them near tomatoes as a preventative measure against pests such as whitefly, and soil nematodes.*

in the chain, destroying the fine, natural balance.

There are several positive steps one can take to enhance the natural process.
• Change your attitude. Do not expect perfection in the garden. Accept that a certain percentage of the crop may be damaged slightly or be eaten by predators.
• Grow only those vegetables, fruit and herbs that will do well in your particular area or climate. These are the ones that will do best.
• Prior to planting, always prepare the

*A simple trick like tying strips of fabric to string stretched over young seedlings will help deter birds from feasting on the crops or digging for worms and uprooting the plants.*

help keep the soil light, friable and healthy.

• Maintain the garden with routine watering, mulching and feeding.

• Keep the area around plants free from weeds, and always clear away fallen fruits which encourage fruit fly the following season. Clean cultivation is vital in the chain of pest prevention.

• Consider using organic fly traps, baits and sprays.

• Keep weed growth clear from the base of plants affected by fungal disease. Good air circulation greatly helps prevent this.

## ORGANIC TIPS

• Manually remove aphids, or spray with a garden hose.

• Shallow saucers of flat beer will attract and kill snails and slugs.

• A fine line of sawdust or holly leaves around the garden bed will deter snails and slugs.

• Throw netting over trees to protect fruit from birds. Aluminium pie-dishes hung in the trees cause reflection, which is also effective.

• Boil rhubarb leaves in water, then dilute this mixture and spray on to plants to discourage aphids and caterpillars.

• Other useful sprays can be made from soap, washing soda and nicotine.

• Pyrethrum-based sprays are effective against a wide range of leaf-chewing insects, and are also environmentally friendly.

• White oil is a harmless spray against scale.

• Sulphur and copper sprays are also safe, and useful against fungal diseases.

soil well, and keep a good supply of organic matter to build up and feed the soil.

• Choose only healthy, robust specimens when planting—weakened plants are susceptible to damage and disease.

• Follow methods such as crop rotation and companion planting.

• Check plants regularly for signs of disease or insect infestation. Do not wait until it is too late.

• Plant species that attract birds to the garden, as many birds will eat insects that may be attacking your garden.

• Encourage earthworms in the soil with homemade compost. These worms will

# *Chemical warfare*

*The following chart is divided into two parts: the first listing pests and the solutions used to eradicate them; the second describing symptoms of various diseases and solutions to use on affected plants.*

| PEST | DESCRIPTION | SOLUTION |
|---|---|---|
| Aphid | Tiny green, yellow or black insects | Dimethoate or demeton-S-methyl |
| Black scale | Soft brown scales on stems | White oil spray |
| Broad mite | Almost invisible | Wettable sulphur or sulphur powder |
| Cabbage moth | Moths that lay eggs on foliage. These hatch into larvae | Dust with carbaryl or dipel spray |
| Cabbage white butterfly | Green larvae that hatch from moth eggs | Dust with carbaryl or maldison |
| Caterpillars | Leaf-eating larvae | Dust with carbaryl |
| Codling moth | Egg-laying moths | Remove infected fruit, then use carbaryl spray |
| Cutworms | Small caterpillars that eat foliage | Dust with carbaryl |
| Earth mites | Tiny red or pink mites | Derris dust and weeding |
| Frosted scale | White powdery wax on stems | White oil spray as directed |
| Fruit flies | Flies that lay eggs beneath fruit skin | Fenthion or dimethoate spray |
| Leaf beetles | Leaf-eating beetles including pumpkin beetle larvae | Avoid spraying; remove manually |
| Mealybugs | Oval insects covered in waxy thread | Demeton-S-methyl as directed |
| Scales | Sap-eating insects on leaf undersides | White oil and maldison mixture |
| Slugs and snails | Leaf-eaters that attack seedlings | Snail pellets |
| Spider mites | Tiny mites that attack conifers | Dicifol as directed |
| Thrips | Almost invisible, appear as specks | Maldison spray as directed |
| Whiteflies | Small white waxy flies | Pyrethrum spray as directed |
| Woolly aphids | Aphids covered in waxy threads | Dimethoate spray as directed |

## CHEMICAL WARFARE (CONT.)

| DISEASE | DESCRIPTION | SOLUTION |
|---|---|---|
| Apple scab | Black spotting on foliage | Copper oxychloride as directed |
| Basal rot | Yellowing of foliage | Immerse bulbs in thiabendazole |
| Black rot | Soil-borne causing yellowing of foliage | Avoid overcrowding; remove damaged plants |
| Black spot | Rose foliage becomes spotted | Create space around plants |
| Brown rot | Fruit become spotted then rots | Copper oxychloride as directed |
| Bulb and stem nematode | Distortion of young foliage, then rot | Destroy affected bulbs |
| Citrus scab | Enlarged fruit; premature falling | Copper oxychloride spray |
| Collar rot | Affects seedlings; foliage yellows | Drench soil with quintozone |
| Damping off | Stem rots then seedling dies | Spray soil with furalaxyl before planting |
| Downy mildew | Downy patches on foliage | Zineb or furalaxyl as directed |
| Grey mould | Grey, furry fungus in humid climates | Destroy diseased plants |
| Leaf blight | Spotted foliage | Zineb or copper oxychloride spray |
| Leaf curl | Distortion and curling of foliage | Copper oxychloride before bud swell |
| Leaf spot | Brown spots on foliage | Zineb or oxychloride spray |
| Mosaic | Mottling of foliage | Remove and destroy affected plants |
| Powdery mildew | Powdery leaf patches, distortion | Dinocap or benomyl spray as directed avoid overcrowding |
| Rust | Yellow patches on upper foliage | Choose resistant varieties |

# Index

# *Acknowledgements*

Thanks are extended to Robert Allsop for the design of the permaculture gardens, Barbara Schreiner (permaculture garden), and Kaye Healey for location research.

## PHOTOGRAPHY CREDITS

*Front cover* Jerry Harpur; *Back cover* Weldon Publishing; *Endpapers* Laurie Greenup; *pp.2–3* Jerry Harpur; *p.4* Diggers' Club; *p.5* Weldon Publishing; *pp.6–7* Mary Moody; *p.8* Weldon Publishing; *p.9* Jerry Harpur; *p.10* Lorna Rose; *p.12* Gil Hanly; *p.13* Mary Moody; *pp.14–15* Cheryl Maddocks; *p.17* Jennie Churchill; *p.20* Gil Hanly; *p.21* Jerry Harpur; *p.23* Weldon Publishing; *p.27* Gil Hanly; *p.29* Weldon Publishing; *p.32* Weldon Publishing; *p.33* Derek Fell; *p.37* Diggers' Club; *p.41* Diggers' Club; *p.43* Gil Hanly; *p.45* Jerry Harpur; *pp.48–49* Weldon Publishing; *p.50* Jerry Harpur; *p.53* Gil Hanly; *p.55* Jerry Harpur; *p.57* Jerry Harpur; *p.58* Mary Moody; *p.59* Lorna Rose; *p.60* Weldon Publishing; *p.61* Derek Fell; *p.63* Lorna Rose; *pp.64–65* Laurie Greenup; *p.66* Gil Hanly; *p.67* Cheryl Maddocks; *p.68* Weldon Publishing; *pp.69,70,72,73,74,75* Laurie Greenup; *p.76* Mary Moody; *p.77* Laurie Greenup; *p.78* Weldon Publishing; *pp.80, 81* Laurie Greenup; *pp.82–83* Weldon Publishing; *p.84* Jerry Harpur; *p.85* Weldon Publishing; *p.87* Andrew Elton/Weldon Publishing; *p.89 top* Ray Joyce/Weldon Publishing; *p.89 bottom* Ray Joyce/Weldon Publishing; *p.91* Ray Joyce/Weldon Publishing; *pp.92,93,94,95,96* Weldon Publishing; *p.96 left* Weldon Publishing; *p.96 right* Reg Morrison/Weldon Publishing; *p.97* Weldon Publishing; *pp. 98–99* Laurie Greenup; *p.100* Mary Moody; *p.101* Colin Beard/Weldon Publishing; *p.103* Cheryl Maddocks; *p.104* Mary Moody; *pp.105,106,107,108,109,110* Laurie Greenup; *p.111* Weldon Publishing; *pp.112–113* Cheryl Maddocks; *p.114* Trisha Dixon; *p.115* Christine Whiston; *p.118* Weldon Publishing; *p.120* Lorna Rose; *p.122* Mary Moody

Published by Lansdowne Publishing Pty Ltd
Level 5, 70 George Street, Sydney NSW 2000, Australia

First published by Weldon Publishing 1992
Reprinted by Lansdowne Publishing Pty Ltd 1995

Managing Director: Jane Curry
Production Manager: Sally Stokes
Publishing Manager: Deborah Nixon
Copy editor: Shirley Jones
Designer: Kathie Baxter Smith
Illustrator: Valerie Price


Designed on Quark Express in 11.5pt Garamond 3
Printed in Singapore by Kyodo Printing Co. (S'pore) Pte Ltd


National Library of Australia Cataloguing-in-Publication data


Moody, Mary
Vegetables, herbs and fruit.

Includes index.
ISBN 1 86302 212 0


1. Vegetable gardening. 2. Herb gardening. 3. Fruit-culture.
I. Title. (Series: Pleasure of gardening).

635

*Cover: Eau de cologne mint, camomile, comfrey and apple mint.*

*Title page: A well-organised formal vegetable garden is a visual treat. Here roses, herbs, veg-
etables and perennials are combined in neatly hedged beds.*

*Opposite contents page: Curved beds of vegetables and herbs as part of a potager garden.*

*Contents page: The flavour and freshness of homegrown vegetables are a great attraction
for many gardeners. Here a crisp head of cabbage (Brassica oleracea var. capitata) is
ready for harvesting.*